Edwin Louis Cole

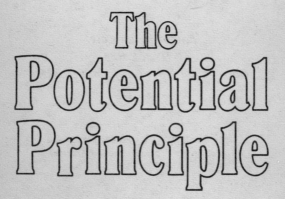

THE POTENTIAL PRINCIPLE

Edwin Louis Cole
P.O. Box 825
Corona del Mar, California 92625

Compiled, arranged, and edited by Donna C. Arthur

Some of the names have been changed to protect the individuals involved. The events are as described.

DEDICATION

Dedicated to the loveliest lady in the land, my wife Nancy, who together with the Lord helps make my dream come true.

My sincere appreciation to Donna Arthur and the staff at Whitaker House who made this book possible.

CONTENTS

Chapter 1

TO DREAM THE IMPOSSIBLE DREAM

I remember when God first spoke to me about changing the direction of my life. Throughout the entire year, He continually spoke to me, reinforcing His will for me. It became a vision, a dream, an impelling force so strong that I left everything I was doing and launched out to do that one thing—to minister to men across the nation and throughout the world.

Dreams are the substances of every great achievement.

Men who dream great dreams sometimes become builders of great edifices such as the Golden Gate Bridge in San Francisco or the Empire State Building in New York. Dreamers develop large cities, construct new nations, and write constitutions.

In spite of opposition, laughter, ridicule, hardship, or persecution, they never lose their dream. Because they never lose their dream, they continue on and become a success in this world by translating their dreams into reality.

God gave Bob Schuller a dream. That dream came to pass, and it is a reality today in the great Crystal Cathedral in Orange County, California.

In spite of what everyone said about it, it is now a world landmark. It is one of the sights that everyone wants to see whenever they visit Southern California, just like Disneyland or Knotts Berry Farm. It's a testimony in itself.

Perhaps there were times when Bob Schuller was going through his own discouragement or persecution. He may have wondered about his vision. But he never lost his dream.

Dreams are important.

The Word of God teaches that it is one of the major ways that God speaks to His men concerning His work.

Everyone has a dream.

It is my purpose in writing this book to help you recognize, retain, or realize your life's dream. As you read the following pages, you will find there are definite principles involved that will help you become one of God's successes.

However, this is not a book about positive thinking or possibility thinking, but about reality thinking because *truth and reality are synonymous.*

Everything God does, He does according to a pattern based upon a principle of His Kingdom. When we act in faith upon one of these Biblical principles, it becomes the key that unlocks heaven's riches to us.

The more we base our life upon principles and less upon personalities, the straighter our course will be.

Using Joseph's life from the Old Testament as a guide, I would like to show you how God develops potential principles in our lives based on the principles of His Kingdom.

God gave Joseph a dream. It was a God-breathed, God-ordained, God-given dream. The dream held the potential for a successful life, blessing and prosperity for others, and salvation for Joseph's family and his nation.

The God-given dream created an image in his mind that would ultimately become a reality. It was real in Joseph's spirit before it became real in his flesh.

Joseph's dream came directly from God.
He never lost his dream.

Scripture teaches that God is the author and finisher of our faith. God will finish what He authors, but He is not obligated to finish what He has not authored.

If God implants His desires in our heart, then He will see to it that they are completed as we submit to His Lordship and work in cooperation with His Spirit within us. That is how His Kingdom is able to come to earth through us.

There is an old adage that says, "Life begins at forty." Forty is generally the time in life when we realize our youth is gone. With it there is an evaluation of what has been done and what is yet to be done in life. The evaluation can become a life-changing event.

It is during this time that many find their dreams fulfilled or unfulfilled. Dreams, goals, priorities, and relationships are all affected.

It is time to redirect, rededicate, or reinforce direction and goals in life.

A dream, when shattered, can be devastating for an individual. This is not a mid-life crisis, but something in the very warp and woof of the nature of man's spirit.

The disappointment of a shattered dream can degenerate into discouragement, then to disillusionment, and often leads to alcoholism, drug addiction, suicide, or even ends in murder.

Dreams that are nothing more than fantasies cannot stand the test of reality.

Ghetto dwellers living a fantasy life through television often become rebellious, antisocial, and anarchistic in their behavior; when the TV is shut off, they are left with the reality of rats, tenements, cold water flats, and poverty.

Without a dream to achieve, they are without hope.

Today's under twenty-five-year-old generation has a slogan that says, "No hope." They are without hope for their generation in this nuclear society.

Without hope, life is hopeless. Faith is the substance of things hoped for. [1]

Without a dream for their generation,

young people have nothing to put their faith in and nothing to base their hope on.

Like Joseph who received a God-given dream in his youth, today's youth need to seek God for their dreams.

In many American homes men and women do not understand each other. Many men have unfulfilled dreams of being a successful husband, father, or businessman. As a result, they have become negative, embittered, critical fault finders. Rather than face the reality of their own failures, they blame their wives, circumstances, environment, or heredity. A wife often suffers the indignities of her husband's inabilities to fulfill his dreams.

Now, with the importance of dreams and their results established, both positive and negative, get a Bible and read the story of Joseph as recorded in the book of Genesis from the thirty-seventh chapter to the end of the fiftieth chapter. You need to read it to understand some of the things I will be referring to.

As you read it, you will see that Joseph's success came from his identification with God, rather than his identification with family or circumstance.

Joseph's dream was God's revelation of leadership.

Every great leader knows there is a price to pay for that leadership, whether in a secular or sacred place of leadership.

Joseph's price was spending thirteen years in intense confrontation with temptation and accusation. This was his testing time and God's proving time.

All testing is based on resistance.

It's a Kingdom principle.

Scripture says, "Submit yourselves therefore to God. Resist the devil, and he will flee from you."[2] It means your ability to resist the devil is proportionate to your submission to the Lord.

It's the reason God's Word encourages men to begin the day seeking the Lord. Without first submitting to the Lord in the morning, men often do not have the ability to resist the devil in the afternoon. Impatience, temper outbursts, or fleshly indulgences often are the products of a lack of submission to the Lord at the beginning of the day.

Joseph was to be a leader. It would take time. Leadership may be birthed in a man, but the quality of it can only be produced over a period of time. Preparation is the foundation for success.

Look at how the Marine Corps, Army, Navy, and Air Force prepare their leaders in "boot camps," then move them to deeper training.

In the technical trades, there is an "apprenticeship" program to prepare men as journeymen craftsmen. One of the problems of modern society is there are many journeymen but few craftsmen. All too often men in our "instant" society manufacture products without quality because of improper preparation. They do not want to pay the price of time.

Even in the ministry there are some men who can handle sermons, some who can handle churches, or some who can handle God's Word—but they can't handle themselves.

Moses failed one time to handle himself and as a result missed Canaan. Adam, David, Samson, all learned that "he that ruleth his spirit (is better) than he that taketh a city."[3]

Joseph believed in his dream, but his brothers did not.

While Joseph identified with God, his brothers identified with their personal desires, ambitions, pleasures, and sin. That was the dichotomy between them and Joseph. It was a chasm or a gulf. They could never understand Joseph. They had an entirely different perspective of life.

When Joseph told his brothers his dream, their jealousy of him turned to hatred. Jealousy is more dangerous and cruel than anger. Jealousy is vicious. And flattery is disguised hostility. Beware of each.

His brothers did not, could not, or would not understand him. They never did. Even after he forgave them, favored them, lavished the largesse of his kindness on them, they still thought that he would wreak vengeance upon them after their father died.

Their portrait of Joseph was colored by their own selfish, lustful, petty spirits. To the pure all things are pure, to the impure is nothing pure.[4] Those words describe them accurately.

Joseph faced jealousy, anger, hatred, envy, and slander. He was betrayed, ignored, rejected, and humiliated. He suffered cruelty, injustice, and evil craftiness. He was the victim of conspiracy, sold down the river by his brothers, imprisoned through false accusations, defrauded by those he befriended. He had to contend against malice and lust allayed against him.

But Joseph persevered. *Perseverance will always outlast persecution.*

You're never too young, too old, too poor, or too rich for God to make your dream a reality. God is not partial, neither is He a respecter of persons.[5] God wants you to have what He has given to others.

Josephs' faith never ended. His life did, but his faith didn't. He made his children promise that, when they returned to the Promised Land, they would carry up his bones with them.

He knew that what God authors, He will finish; what God promises, He will fulfill; what's committed to Him, He will keep.

That's what made Joseph a hero of faith. It's what will make you a hero of faith.

God wants you to be a hero of faith.

Faith overcomes the world.

Believe God to make your dream a reality.

God-given dreams in God-favored men make a God-blest world.

Chapter 2

MARCHING TO A DIFFERENT DRUMMER

Some men "happen" to influence while others "determine" to do it. This is the difference between a follower and a leader.

That's why Joseph is so admirable. He was a spiritual achiever, the Bible calls such people *overcomers.*

Mediocre men settle for good which often is the enemy of best.

Joseph pursued excellence. His life was filled with the transcendent glory of God. It was this glory that helped develop his potential.

God gives grace to sinners, but He gives glory to saints.

With Joseph it all started with a dream. His God-given dream became a reality because of three things in his life. These are the same three things that all of us need. They are favor, wisdom, and courage.

It was written of the Lord Jesus Christ when here on earth that He grew in wisdom and favor with God and man.[1] Joseph is an Old Testament type of Jesus.

Joseph's authority and ability were the result of God's favor. He incurred favor with God and man, but he never tried to curry it. He merited men's favor, but God's favor is always bestowed as a gift and can never be earned. That's why it's called grace, which means unmerited favor.

His desire was for rightness. Such rightness given by God's grace is righteousness.

He certainly was not trying to gain favor with his father when he told him about the evil his brothers were doing. That was simply an evidence of his prophetic nature and gift.

All prophets have a highly developed sense of justice, deploring injustice, and are given to exposing sin. That's why God uses prophets. To call people back to righteousness and awaken in them a God-consciousness is the prophet's basic ministry.

Joseph's favor with God was evidenced by the fact that everything he did, God made it to prosper. Joseph's favor with his father was evidenced by the "coat of many colors."[2]

In describing a man like Joseph the Psalmist said, "and whatsoever he doeth shall prosper."[3]

God is for prosperity and against poverty.

Everywhere he went, Joseph rose to a place of leadership. No matter how humbly he may have started, whether at home, Potiphar's house, or prison, he eventually was elevated to a place of leadership.

It is axiomatic that "water will always seek it's own level."

It's a principle of life.

You will always live to the level of your faith. Not everyone lives on the same level of faith. As your faith rises to different levels, or your business rises, or your income rises, you will always be in a shifting pattern of relationships and friendships. Intimate friendships change at each level. That is part of the price of growth.

It's also the reason why some people don't grow. They allow their intimate friends to influence them against growing in grace. Because their friends have not experienced new levels of truth, or experienced a fresh manifestation of God's presence through hunger to know God, they discourage those who have that hunger.

If God has lifted you to a new level of faith through revelation, experience, or relationship with God, you cannot afford to let those who have not risen to that new level hold you back and keep you from growing and maturing.

Martin Luther would never have been the catalyst for the reformation if he had listened to his companions who could not understand the revelation that "the just shall live by faith."[4]

Men, whether ministers or laymen, have a tendency to be intimidated by other men's philosophies that are nothing more than rationalizations

17

to justify failures. When you accept such philosophies, you accept the failures upon which they are based.

For years I was a consultant to major ministries and businesses across America. One of the distinguishing characteristics of many who were unhappy and disgruntled was that the ministry or business they were in grew, but they did not.

As a result, they became negative in their feelings.

Or, if men grew and the ministry or business didn't, they would eventually outgrow it and have to leave.

Ministries also grow to the level of their leaders.

Put a man in a congregation with a hundred people when he has the spirit and capacity to pastor a thousand, and the congregation will grow to a thousand. Put a man in a congregation with a thousand who has the spirit and ability to pastor only a hundred, and the congregation will soon be reduced to that.

Along the way, intimate friendships change with the authority and ability of the leadership. Which means, you don't cut off old friends, you just keep making new ones on a higher level of faith. Your association and intimacy with people will change as you grow and mature.

There are only two things you do in life.

You enter and leave.

Whether it is a school, an organization, a

friendship, or a business, that's basically all you do your entire life. That's why *how you leave* one often determines *how you enter* another.

Ministers need to know that. It's the reason people need to always leave church blessed in spirit, for then they will desire to enter again.

Wives need to know that about their husbands and children when they leave for work or school in the morning.

God wants to change us by pouring out our lives from glory to glory. Don't let someone else's unbelief, rejection of truth, or refusal to grow stop your life or your dream.

Grow with God. Grow in grace. Grow in truth.

Joseph's growth in wisdom came from several sources. He received it from his father Jacob, his grandfather Isaac, and his great-grandfather Abraham. He esteemed the wisdom of his fathers.

The writings available to Joseph, and God's Spirit within him, gave him wisdom.

Joseph's ability to interpret dreams was best summed up by Pharoah when he said, "Can we find such a one as this is, a man in whom the Spirit of God is?"[5]

One of Joseph's descendents in faith would write one day, "Wisdom is the principal thing; therefore get wisdom."[6]

One of the wisest men who ever lived, King Solomon, said repeatedly in Proverbs that wisdom gives a long good life, riches, honor, pleasure, and peace. In other words, wisdom provides for the totality of a man's life.

And Joseph experienced them all.

Wisdom will bring you the same thing if you pursue it. That is why the Word of God is so important in your life, because Christ is made unto us— "Wisdom." Devotion to Him and His Word will cause us to become men of wisdom.

Wisdom, like peace, must be sought after. It is like time, you don't find time—you take time.

The potential for developing wisdom is available to us, but we must invest time for its development. The potential for developing wisdom will be impaired or lost by the way we use our time. Time spent in foolishness will never develop wisdom.

Meditation in God's Word is the matrix of creativity.

God required of Moses that he build a fence around the base of the mount where he had gone up to meet with God. The fence was to keep wild animals from intruding. We must learn to discipline our minds to keep the wild thoughts from intruding into our peace in the presence of God.

It takes time to be holy, wise, or proficient.

You can regain wealth or health, but you can never regain time that has been lost. Regret will never turn back a clock.

Favor, wisdom, and courage were the elements that contributed so mightily to Joseph's success.

He added courage to his faith.

Heroes are men in whom courage has become visible. *Heroes are men who act from a need greater than self.*

Whether from Joseph, or from Jairus who sought Jesus for the healing of his daughter, it is true in every life. Ordinary men who, in a moment of time, act from a need greater than self become heroes. Courage makes it possible.

We need courage to face reality.

We need courage to admit need.

We need courage to make decisions.

We need courage to change.

We need courage to hold convictions.

Since the time of Adam's first "cover-up" in the garden, men have attempted to avoid accountability for what they've done and escape from the reality of themselves. Philosophies, ideologies, drugs, suicide, and many other assorted methods are used to evade reality.

One of the hardest things for a person to admit is that he is wrong. Yet it's the first step toward maturity or a solution to prodigal problems.

Heroes are ordinary men who act in a moment of time on a need greater than themselves.

The saying, "It takes a great man to admit he's wrong," is old but true.

Joseph gave God something in his life to

work with, and God gave Joseph something in his life to work for.

It's a two-way street.

If you want God to develop the potential of your life, then you not only need God to give you something, but you need to give God something.

Give God your time.

Let Him give you His transcendent glory.

Let God develop your potential.

Chapter 3

YOUR LIFE HAS POTENTIAL

Some time ago I heard the story of the inventor who developed a pin curl clip that made him a fortune. What he had done was take two little pieces of metal; and by a very simple but ingenious method of putting them together, he caused a spring action. It is used today as an instrument to pin curls together for styling women's hair.

What he had done was put time, ingenuity, creativity, expertise, and effort into those two little pieces of metal. From it he made himself a fortune and life easier for women all over the world.

Or how about the man who used to fold the corners of his papers with a slight tear and bend to hold them together for filing. His desire to find a better way resulted in the invention of the paper clip.

All he had done was take a little piece of wire about three inches long and twisted it into a certain shape. It was a little piece of wire that you and I would throw away. But he took it and made a paper clip giving him a fortune and blessing the lives of countless clerks all over the world.

The story I really like is one I heard years ago in a motivational lecture.

It was about the man who called a soft drink dispensing company years ago when they were still serving from counters at drug stores. He told the executive committee that he had something that would make them a fortune, but he wanted $75,000 for it.

The story goes that when the entire Board of Directors met to hear him, he simply walked in and said two words, "Bottle it." From that, it was stated, the company went around the world in business.

Experience, emotions, ideas, wood, salt, land, talent, beauty, brains all have one thing in common. Potential.

How can we forget the time when our Lord wanted to feed a multitude and all that was near was a little boy with a few fish and loaves of bread. It is written that the Lord Jesus, took those, blessed them, and brake them, and used them to feed a multitude.[1]

All the fish and loaves had was potential until Jesus put something into them, then they were used to feed a multitude.

The exchange of breathing develops the potential of your lungs to continue to give you life. So does the process of the blood pumping through your body to every cell in it, taking in food and carrying away waste.

Exchange is the process of life.

One of the common errors that many people make about God's creative ability stems from the fact that they misconstrue Scripture to say that God made everything from nothing. Paraphrased, the Scripture says, "By faith—by believing God—we know that the world and the stars—in fact, all things—were made at God's command; and that they were all made from things that can't be seen."[2]

There it is.

Something isn't made from nothing—it is made from things that are not seen. Everyone knows that the true value of anything is internal, not external. Things that cannot be seen which are eternal are far more important than the things that can be seen which are temporal.

The house I live in is built of wood, mortar, glass, metal, and other assorted materials. That is the visible part. But what was put into it to make it all a reality cannot be seen. Someone put into this property vision, faith, ingenuity, knowledge, talent, and effort. None of which can be seen visibly, only the result can be seen.

It's the same with a marriage.

The other day I had the privilege of being in a city where I met a very fine looking middle-aged couple. They were obviously appreciative of each other and openly told of the wonderful marriage they were enjoying.

In talking with them, they said it was not always that way. But after many years of putting caustic comments, bitterness, resentment, and hostility into their marriage, and only getting out of it unhappiness and misery, they made a decision to change.

He made the first step. He began to show appreciation, kindness, and gentility toward her. He began to communicate and listen to her. Out of this action, she began to respond and change also. What they put into their marriage determined what they got out.

Marriage is the closest thing to a heaven or hell there is in this life it seems. Putting negatives into a marriage produces hardship and hellishness.

This principle centers in the Cross of Christ. Salvation for man exists in reality, but only has potential until an exchange is made. God took the sinless Christ and poured into Him our sins. Then, in exchange, He poured God's goodness into us.

Jesus came in His righteousness and became identified with our sins so that we, through repentance and faith, could become identified with His righteousness. Please understand, if all you do is admit He came and did His part, but you have never completed that process of exchange by doing your part, then Calvary only holds the potential for your being saved. You are yet without the reality of it.

Not the hearers, but the doers will be possessors.

The other day I was riding with a man in his car when he pointed out a piece of property and said, "I could have bought that fifteen years ago for only $3,000 and now it's worth $130,000." He didn't impress me. He was no closer to owning it now than he was then. He was a talker, not a doer.

Why?

Because he did not have in his spirit the faith, courage, vision, acumen to make it come to pass. He had never developed much of the potential of his life because he had not put enough into it.

Some men make their dreams come true by what they exchange to bring it into reality. Others just moan because they don't have the material, money, or means to begin. Successful men begin where they are with what they have.

Consider the spiritual achievers recorded in the Bible.

They overcame their lack in material things by what they had in their spirit.

Elisha only had a pinch of salt, but putting what he had in his spirit into it—his faith in God—he used the pinch of salt to make the bitter waters sweet.

And what about Gideon's pitchers, Samson's

jawbone of an ass, or Moses' rod. It was not what was in their hand, but what was in their heart that made the difference.

The Philharmonic director can get beautiful music from his orchestra; but when he started music instruction as a boy, he began with one hand on a piano keyboard doing scales. He grew into his knowledge by putting all he had into it.

Hear this. *Faith and fear both attract.*

Faith is believing that what you cannot see will come to pass. Fear is believing that what you cannot see will come to pass.

Faith attracts the positive; fear attracts the negative.

Two young boys visiting with their parents at a home reacted differently to the little Chihauhau dog that lived there. One loved it and in faith petted and played with it. The other was afraid and ultimately was bitten by the dog. It obviously illustrates the principle by which faith and fear attract.

This very reason is why I am concerned about some people who are engaged in the "nuclear-freeze" movement. It's not that I am concerned about those who genuinely want peace, because I, too, am a man of peace. It's the reason that today I'm still involved as Chairman of the "Committee for International Good Will."

However, "Freeze-niks" motivated by fear will attract attack from our enemies, and then where will the peace be?

A recent poll showed that people with a poor self-image tend to suffer far greater abuse and misuse than those with a positive self-image. The inference was that those with negative attitudes from poor self-images seemed to attract the abuse while those with a positive attitude repelled it.

Job said it best when he said, "For the thing which I greatly feared is come upon me."[3]

Often it is necessary to make drastic decisions and do traumatic things to assure a change in how others see us or regard us.

Joseph's change from the time his brothers last saw him in the pit where they left him to when they saw him again as a ruler in Egypt was dramatic and traumatic. Yet through it all, Joseph lived a life of positive spirituality. He was being constantly renewed in the spirit of his mind.

Joseph grew, matured, changed, and became every inch the leader God intended him to be. His brothers found it hard to realize who he had become by the fulfillment of the dream God gave him.

He was not limited in his life by how others saw or regarded him. He did not limit the Holy One of Israel in his life by allowing someone else to create his world for him.

Joseph was a man of faith with a God-given dream. His dream only had the potential of coming true, but when he put faith into his dream, it became a reality.

Don't limit God.

Let God develop your potential.

Begin with what you have.

Identify with God and what God says.

Be strong in faith.

Renew the spirit of your mind with God's Word.

Repeat this out loud: "I am who God says I am, I have what God says I have, and I can do what God says I can do, because God's grace is sufficient in my life."

Chapter 4

CONVERT YOUR NEGATIVES
TO POSITIVES

God ends everything on the positive. God never ends anything on the negative.

Joseph's life is both an evidence and a testimony to that truth.

God always creates in perfection. When God created us in Adam, we were made perfect in our humanity. Adam was a perfect human being, without sin and without blight.

God put Adam in the Kingdom of God and the Kingdom of God in Adam when He placed him in Eden. When God completed His work in creation, He saw that it was good and rested from His work.

From then until now, *peace has always been the umpire for doing the will of God.*

We were created for God's pleasure. Therefore, fellowship with God was the normal way for Adam to live. He walked and talked with God.

When Adam sinned, everything changed. All human nature changed from positive to negative.

Even the earth became negative by entering into the curse as a result of sin.

Adam's expulsion from Eden was symbolic of his expulsion from the Kingdom of God as a result of his sin. Everything in human society became perverted as a result of Adam's sin.

Now, everything in life must be converted from negative to positive.

Even the ground must be converted by being cultivated, planted, and watered. Left to itself, in its negative state, it will only grow wild with weeds.

There is a story about a man in one of the Scandinavian countries who was an extremely rich man. He died. In his will he left all his property to the devil. Having no living relatives, his will went to probate court. He became a very publicized man. The newspapers carried it and wondered what kind of a decision the judge would make. How can material things be given to the devil?

When the day came that he was to issue his edict, the court was absolutely crowded. The judge banged the gavel and began reading the will. He said, "It is the decision of this court that the proceeds of this estate be used to build a fence around this owner's property and that guards be maintained on a twenty-four hour vigil so that no one ever again sets foot on this property."

Court was dismissed and everybody walked away. No one could understand what he meant by that. All of a sudden everyone understood. *Things left to themselves naturally go to the devil.*

Parents never have to teach their children to disobey. Disobedience is natural to negative human nature. All humanity is negative by nature. We must learn to obey.

One of the basic principles of the Kingdom of God is that all the characteristics of the Kingdom emanate from the character of the King. Thus, all the characteristics of God's Kingdom are positive, because all of the attributes and virtues of God are positive.

Contrary to that, all of the characteristics of the kingdom of Satan are negative, because his character is negative.

Light, life, love, truth, honor, and faith are all characteristics of the Kingdom of God and are all positive.

Darkness, death, lust, lying, dishonor, and fear all belong in a kingdom where Satan rules.

Righteousness is always positive. Sin is always negative.

That's why conversion is necessary to human life.

Because we are negative by nature, conditioned to failure in this world and subject to sin, we must be converted in all areas of our life. Even our attitudes, habits, thought patterns, emotions, relationships, and appetites must be constantly converted.

It's the reason children will never ask their

parents for something only one time. They know the natural answer will be negative, so they ask until parents are converted from negative to positive.

The same principle holds true for salesmen. They know their initial response from a client will generally be negative. Sales motivation clinics teach how to convert the client from negative to positive.

Buyer's remorse sometimes occurs when a person buys while he is still in a negative frame of mind, causing him to want to return the item for a refund.

This is not uncommon to ministers either. Listen to successful ministers pray. They generally begin with a confession before God of who they are in Christ. They thank Him for what He has done in their lives, praise Him for what He will do as His Word goes forth, and acknowledge Him for the signs, wonders, and miracles that will occur.

Expectancy is the atmosphere for miracles.

To create an atmosphere of expectancy is to prepare for success.

Oral Roberts does that with his very first greeting. "Something good is going to happen to you!" Immediately he creates an atmosphere of expectancy. He does it with positive words of faith, declaring the goodness of God.

Consider the man whose mother woke him in the morning to go to church, and he said he was not going. When his mother asked why, he answered emphatically, "Those people don't like me, I feel lonely there, and besides no one ever listens to me."

Then he turned to his mother and asked why she thought he ought to go. Her reply was simple and straightforward.

"First of all," she said, "that is not true; second, they do like you; and third, you're the pastor."

An old joke you say. But how successful are other men who have the same kind of attitude about their work, the people they work with, or people in general?

Everyone has to be converted from the negative to the positive.

Even you.

For thirteen years Joseph went through one negative circumstance after another. But he kept a positive attitude of faith. He never lost his dream.

He kept constant communication with God. Communication is the basis of life. When communication stops, abnormality sets in. The ultimate end of abnormality is death, unless there is reconciliation and renewed communication.

A flower will constantly produce as long as it abides in the stem and the stem in the plant. Once it is severed and communication stops, abnormality sets in, and it withers and dies.

That process is in everything in life whether it's in plant life or human relationships.

In the parable of the prodigal son, Jesus gives us the pattern of humanity. The parable is more than just a story about a young boy who runs away from home. In it Jesus gives us the very definitive, basic teaching of the story of humanity from God's perspective. The pattern is rebellion, ruin, repentance, reconciliation, and restoration.

Repentance is the pivotal point between ruin and reconciliation.

When the prodigal broke off communication with his father and separated himself, he began to live an abnormal life. Only when he came to himself and repented was he able to restore communication which led to reconciliation and complete restoration.

God wants your life to end on a positive also.

If you've lost communication through sin, then repent, be reconciled to God, and let God restore you to your proper place in His Kingdom through Jesus Christ our Lord.

God can do it in every area of your life.

At a retreat in Colorado Springs, a man came to me after the services and with much emotion told me the following story.

"My daughter has been gone from home for seven years. I came here with the director of Teen Challenge. The director thought I needed this retreat before I meet my daughter next week.

"Seven years ago she left home, and for seven years I have blamed her, been angry with

36

her, denied her, and rejected her. She's been on drugs, been involved in prostitution, and done every other kind of thing you can think of. I felt as though she had humiliated and embarrassed me. Mine was a very negative attitude.

"Tonight, God revealed to me that her rebellion was not her fault but mine. While in school, she wanted contact lenses instead of glasses in order to look better. When I bought them for her, I told her if she lost them I wouldn't get her any more. Sure enough, three days after having them, she lost them down the drain in the bathroom. When she asked for another pair, I refused. She begged. She cried. She tried every way in the world to get me to buy her another pair, and I rejected her every entreaty.

"Two days later, she asked again. I rejected her request again. She took off the glasses, threw them on the ground, and stomped on them. I was infuriated. I told her if she was willing to do that she could go to school without any glasses. She did, but the following day when she went to school, she never came home.

"For seven years she has been gone. All this time I have felt as though she was at fault. Until tonight. God has finally opened my eyes, and I had the courage to face reality, admit my need as well as my sin, and to ask God to forgive me—not her—and to bring a reconciliation and restoration of our relationship.

"Ed, God has worked a miracle in my life,

and I can hardly wait to see my daughter next week and bring her back to where she belongs.''

He was a success. An achiever. But he had to repent, to go from ruin to reconciliation. It was worth it. Now he not only walks and talks with God, but God has made it possible for him to live a normal life with his daughter.

There are many ways men can become successful. Success is in many areas of our lives.

God has made it possible for the same thing to happen in your life.

Trust God to do it today.

Chapter 5

CHARACTER BUILDING BLOCKS

Watergate was a watershed in American history. It revealed the authority of the Constitution of the United States in a way that had never been seen before. Men's characters were revealed in relationship to it.

Probably Jeb McGruder, who was involved in it, summed it up best when he said, "We were willing to subvert our own moral character to the character of the group, and we went down the tubes in the process. I cannot justify it, but I can say that it was not unique. There were thirty-eight people involved in Watergate. Most of them were very competent, well-to-do lawyers and businessmen, all with good motives. We didn't come to Washington to commit crimes, but we did."[1]

Because we are a people of externalities, we can easily be conditioned to failure by environment or circumstances.

God's Word says, "commit thou to faithful men, who shall be able to teach others also."[2] The principle is that we are to look for character in our leaders and God will add the ability.

We pay millions to movie stars, athletes, and rock artists, many of whom have ungodly characters. Then we complain when some pastor, evangelist, or minister who is earnestly endeavoring to instill eternal and moral values into our society gets a decent income.

Pastors who are doing a real work for God should be the best paid people in the world.

It is true though that some pastors fail to be fishers of men for one simple reason. No fisherman ever cleans his fish before he catches them, and many ministers try to do just that.

Years ago my mother taught me something I have never forgotten. She told me, "Son, there are some people who are better by nature than others are by grace."

Churches often give positions of responsibility to men of talent or ability, and then frustrate themselves attempting to produce character in them. Faithfulness is the cornerstone for building character, family, business, and church.

For God to use you, all you need to have is that one requisite—faithfulness. God will provide you with ability.

Joseph had that one overriding quality of faithfulness.

It is said of Joseph's grandfather Abraham that everywhere God led him, he built his altar and pitched his tent. Today too many men are building their tents and pitching their altars, putting the premium on the material and not the spiritual.

People often major in minors.

The world puts a premium on talent and not character. This is why we must constantly be converted in our thinking, so that we will not succumb to the negative.

Joseph's dream came from God when he was seventeen. He would not have been able to receive it if he had not been in a right relationship with God.

Age has nothing to do with hearing God, but relationship has everything to do with it. Both Eli and Samuel were in the house of worship, and Samuel was only a child while Eli was an aged man. Samuel heard God's voice, Eli didn't. The difference wasn't their age; it was their relationship to God.

Joseph was receptive to revelation. His brothers were not. As he listened to his father tell of the covenant relationship between Jacob's father Isaac and his father Abraham, he assimilated it all into his spirit. Knowledge is like food—it's not how much you get, but how much you assimilate that counts.

There are four distinct periods of Joseph's life: at home, in Potiphar's house, in prison, and as Prime Minister in Egypt.

His entire life was one crisis after another. God would use the crises to develop Joseph's character. Crisis is normal to life, not abnormal. It's the process that is used to take us from a transient to a more permanent situation or relationship.

Sorrow is life's greatest teacher.

In all of it, Joseph's submission was not to the circumstances, but to the God of transcendent glory who was able to take each sorrow and ultimately make it work for Joseph's good.

By His transcendent glory, God was able to take Joseph from prison and place him in the mansion of the Prime Minister. God is able to take a wino from the gutter, save and sanctify him, and make him a great evangelist. God is able to take a prostitute who has been demonically controlled, deliver and cleanse her, and make her an example of faith to other women. God is able to take things that are not and make them into things that are, for His glory.

What God did for Joseph, he can do for you. God can take your life, just as it is, make something special of it, and bring glory to His Name.

Joseph was genuine in his desire for God.

He was so favored even by his father that his father had a special coat made for him. Every time his brothers saw it, they envied him. They mistook his desire to hear spiritual things from his father as a desire to curry favor.

When Joseph told his father the evil his brothers were doing, they regarded him the same way prisoners do a "squealer."

When Joseph told his brothers his dream they decided to get rid of him. The thought of Joseph ruling over them was more than they could take.

Later Joseph would be able to say to them, "Ye thought evil against me, but God meant it for good."[3] They looked on the outward appearances of things, Joseph looked on the internal.

The value of anything is always internal rather than external.

Much is required from those to whom much is given. This is a Kingdom principle because those with authority have a greater responsibility.

God never gives authority without accountability.

My son Paul called me one day and asked my advice about an investment. He began to relate to me the names of all the investors in the venture and was trying to impress me with the investment's value based on the credibility of those he named.

I said, "Son, you don't invest in companies, you invest in men. Who is running the company?"

"I don't know," was his reply.

"Then don't invest until you know who is running the company. Investors are only as good as the men they are investing in."

"But look at all the people that are in it," he countered.

"Doesn't mean a thing. Their money is only as good as the men running the company. You are

43

not investing in the reputation of investors, you are investing in the character of the men running the company,'' I emphasized.

Character is always more important than talent.

God's investment in you is for eternity.

Your value to God is in the Christlikeness of your character.

Chapter 6

IMAGE, IMAGE ON MY MIND

Images—created in us by words, facts, feelings.

One of the most powerful things you can do in life is to create an image. The next most powerful thing you can do is destroy it.

Joseph's God-given dream established an image in his mind of who he was and who he was to become.

We are motivitated to become what we imagine ourselves to be.

We are told that two-thirds of our lifetime impressions are made before we are seven years old. Most of life's basic knowledge, such as the ability to read and write, is given to us before we are ten years old. This is why American educators can give college aptitude tests before students are thirteen years of age.

In reality, the formative years of our lives as children bear on us when we become older. Adult problems more often than not stem from our childhood.

Ninety percent of all child abusers in America were abused themselves as children. Later statistics have indicated one hundred percent in some instances.

It is true. What happens to us in our early years creates images and causes us anxiety, stress, and tension later in life.

It's true in all of us.

Every image created has the potential for good or harm.

A recent letter in response to one of our radio programs was from a young lady who wrote, "Please tell the fathers how their influence can affect their children's lives.

"When my father came home from church, he would sit and watch football. He would comment on the cheerleaders. It was the only time I heard him say nice things about women. So I began to dress like them and act sexy so I would gain my father's approval.

"But it led to sexual promiscuity and all manner of trouble for me. I had an image of what I thought I should be, but I was wrong."

When we teach children to discern right from wrong, it is vital that we do it correctly. When a child reared by a godly parent brings home a swear word from school or from a neighbor, the mother's reaction can last a lifetime.

Overreacting and overstating the issue to insure the child will not use that word again, she says, "Don't ever use that word again, or God won't love you." Later when the child uses the word again, he thinks God doesn't love him so why bother. He throws off all restraint to the use of profanity.

At puberty, when sex is discovered and masturbation becomes a fact of life, parents rightfully desire to discourage its becoming habitual. More than one mother has told her son, "Don't do that or you will commit the unpardonable sin." Now, she may not say it is, but the way she conveys it, she creates an image in the mind of that young person that if he does it, it *is* the unpardonable sin.

Thus when it happens again, the rationale is that having done it, he has committed the unpardonable sin. Therefore, why even try to serve God since he feels he is already lost.

Satan really has but two weapons in his arsenal. Temptation and accusation. When he can't get someone through temptation, he will by accusation.

The accusation of having committed the unpardonable sin is common to all men. Almost all guilt has in it that quality. That's why it is so important to create by words, facts, and feelings the right images.

One of the common ministries for all counselors is to tear down old images that have been created and constructed in the negative, and recreate and reconstruct in the positive.

Every parent needs to understand the principle that new construction is always easier than reconstruction.

Many parents wonder why their children act the way they do when they are the ones who created the distance or aloofness to God by the image they have created in their child's mind.

Children whose image of God comes from dank, dark, unkept church classrooms, and inept, prayerless, and unprepared teachers tend to have severe spiritual problems in relating to God.

As ministers, we often create more anxiety than we do peace in people. We convey by word, gesture, and spirit an image of God and His attitude toward us. Some even make people think they are going to hell because of what they do, instead of what they don't do.

Jesus taught in parables in order to create images. He knew they would become motivational factors in the lives of those who heard Him.

This is why television is such a powerful medium. Radio lets us create our own images, but television does it for us.

We've all watched old romantic movies where the boy and girl chase each other until finally they come to an agreement, he proposes— she accepts. As they embrace with a lover's kiss, up comes the music, and the credits begin their roll with—"THE END".

When two people marry, it's not the end, not by a long shot. It's only the beginning, and every married person knows it. But an image from television has been created.

Many Christians think that when they are saved, it's the end of all their problems. The fact is we are saved, being saved, and will be saved. It's an ongoing process that begins in a moment, but develops in an eternity.

The truth is that, having been born again, instead of living in a one-dimensional world of the flesh, you're now living in a two-dimensional world of flesh and spirit. Sometimes there are *more* problems than there were before.

Before we didn't know what or who was causing our problems, now as Christians we do. Plus now we have a Savior who will deliver us out of them *all!*

Renewing the spirit of your mind is a viable and real process of spiritual life. In it there is a constant renewing, upgrading, and establishing of the images of God, ourselves, and others that is spiritually healthy.

When you change an image, you change behavior, and changing behavior changes feelings.

Those who succeed in life have healthy self-images, and those who fail have poor self-images. That is not just a psychological teaching, but a Kingdom principle directly from the Word of God.

The image in your mind that you have of God is more important than your own.

Jesus Christ came in person to change people's understanding of God. The teachers of God's law had piled so many human interpretations on top of interpretations that God's revelation of Himself to men had become warped, diffused, and distorted. That's what all the fuss was about between Jesus and the Pharisees.

God wants us to know Him personally. Intimately.

If your image of God is given to you by sermons, denominational traditions, doctrines of men, or someone's own personal experiences, you're going to have a problem. Or you already have one.

I've told ministers across the nation to avoid being intimidated in their ministries by other men's philosophies of religion.

I know what it can do. I've seen it in my own life and the lives of others.

I'll never forget when a certain denominational official was teaching young ministers about church growth procedures. His philosophy was that any time a church grew to one hundred members, it should begin immediately to foster another church in the town.

He said that ten churches of one hundred in a town was better than one church with a thousand.

Wrong, wrong, wrong, wrong, wrong.

He had developed that philosophy through a rationalization to justify his own feelings of inadequacy, and now he was passing his failure on to other young men.

Later, I found that he had never pastored a church with more than a hundred people. He went to the mission field where the same thing occurred; and now back at home in an influential position, this was the philosophy he was advocating.

It's the Saul syndrome.

Saul tried to kill David because the people were singing that Saul had killed his thousands, but David his ten thousands. Saul's jealousy raged against David. Saul could not stand the thought of David outdoing him.

The image of David becoming greater than Saul was motivating him toward trying to destroy David.

Don't allow someone else to either create an image of failure or destroy an image of success.

Battling the imposition of others' images of what we should be, or what the Lord's church should be, is a lifelong process.

It's the reason we must daily seek God's Word for ourselves and have the Holy Spirit stamp on our minds and hearts the truths of His Word, so that those images come from God and not men.

It is Jesus Christ who died for our sins, shed His blood, and was raised from the dead to redeem us unto God. It's His church, His truth, His Spirit, His life. All His.

This was brought forcibly home one evening in Denver where hundreds of men had gathered for the rally where I was speaking. I still remember the words vividly.

"If you're here tonight," I preached, "and you are a member of the Board of your congregation, insisting that your church be created according to the image you have in your mind of what it should be, not letting the Holy Spirit create and recreate, then I have a word for you.

"You're dealing with the church for which Christ gave His life, and you're not dealing with a man. You can't deal with it as if it were a business. You can use business methods in many ways, but it's still His church.

"If you're here and will not allow for changes to take place to reach your community for Christ, if you are insisting that the same methods, procedures, time schedules, and traditions be used because that is the way it was when you came into the church, then you are in danger of making the Word of God have no effect by your tradition.

"The message never changes, but the method does. If you are insisting that things be done according to your image of how it should be, and not allowing God to be the Creator, then I have a word for you, and here it is.

"Resign."

What should really count in your life is not what you or others think, but what God is thinking.

To have God pleased with you and to carry that image in your mind is glory.

Chapter 7

THE WAY UP IS DOWN

"And whosoever of you will be the chiefest, shall be servant of all"[1] is the principle of greatness that Jesus gave us. It's a Kingdom principle.

Leadership is not just standing up and yelling, *"Charge!"*

We are only qualified to lead to the degree we are willing to serve. The more we serve the greater we become.

One television network is greater than the others because it serves the greater number of households. One motor company is greater than the others because it serves more customers. Central Church in Seoul, Korea is great because it has two hundred thousand members. The more they serve, the greater they become.

Jesus said how we cared for others would be the measure of our own greatness.

A father's greatness with his family is based on his care for them. His ability to lead is based on his willingness to serve them.

Serving is not servitude. Servitude is bondage. Serving is a voluntary subscription of love.

Love is a characteristic of the Kingdom of God. Lust is a characteristic of Satan's kingdom.

Love is the desire to benefit others at the expense of self, while lust is the desire to benefit self at the expense of others.

Love desires to give. Lust desires to get.

Love serves others. Lust serves self.

Joseph was a loving man; his brothers were lustful. Joseph loved God, while Potiphar's wife lusted after Joseph.

Two thirds of all the basic motives in the world are the lust of the flesh and the lust of the eye. The other third is the pride of life.

Parents are leaders.

When King Solomon ascended to the throne of his father David, he asked for and was given wisdom from the Lord. The first revelation of this wisdom took place when two women were brought before him. Each claimed a living baby was theirs, and the child that had died during the night each disclaimed.

It was the word of each woman against the other. No one could prove or disprove either claim.

Finally, with the wisdom of the Lord, Solomon had the child brought and issued a command to "Divide the living child in two, and give half to the one, and half to the other."[2] The mother who had lusted her child and overlaid it in the night so that it died agreed to take half a child.

The mother who loved her child cried out, "No, let her have the child." When Solomon heard that, he ordered the child given to her. Her willingness to give was an evidence of her love.

Both love and lust were revealed to me in a most remarkable way through the life of a man named Bob. He was good looking, successful in business, popular in the community, excellent in sports, and failing in marriage.

A man can succeed in one area of his life, but fail in another. God wants us to maintain a balance in all we do.

For fourteen years of marriage, he thought the problems he and his wife were having were all her fault. He constantly encouraged her to attend Bible studies, prayer meetings and anything else where he thought she could get help.

He was the leader in the home.

He thought he was exercising his leadership in his home by sending her to get help, not realizing he was the one who needed it.

Then, at a seminar, God spoke to Bob.

Three months after Bob attended the meeting, Bob confessed to me what had happened in his life.

"Ed, it's real," he said. "All these years I thought everything was my wife's fault. Then, at that seminar, when I heard about love and lust, it hit me. All this time I had been lusting my wife, not loving her.

"All I wanted was for her to please me. All I wanted was my own satisfaction. All *I* wanted— Man, was I lustful. Not mean lustful, but selfish lustful, just wanting all I could get, but not giving anything to her.

"Today I've got all I want. All the love and sex I want. Right now I've got to be one of the most blest men alive. I've learned to love. Isn't it great! Thank God I learned before it was too late for me, like it has been for some others."

Putting love into leadership instead of lust developed a whole new life for him. He became a leader through love, by learning to serve.

Love has a lifting power. It elevates.

I heard Charles Capps give a worthy statement one time, "I'm not practicing what I preach, I'm preaching what I practice," he said.

It's not whether we know it or say it, but it's whether we live it that counts.

There are four levels we can live on in life:

On the basis of *assumption,* but assumption is life's lowest level of knowledge.

On the basis of *knowledge*, which comes from facts. We can know it, but not do it, so what good is it doing us?

On the basis of *skills* which is the ability to put knowledge into action. Doing something once, however, doesn't cause it to become part of our way of life.

On the basis of *practice*, which is the highest learning level. To be effective, it must be part of our lifestyle. Leadership is lived on this level.

Every leader or teacher is limited by three things in his life:

The *knowledge* of his own mind.

The *worth* of his own character.

The *principles* upon which he is building his own life.

Athletes are America's princes. By virtue of their visibility and ability, they are supposedly leaders of other men. All their feats are written about in heroic form. Like it or not, they lead our youth by their example.

How devastating then to read of their involvement in drugs, arrest, guilt, sentencing, and imprisonment. All their protestations that their private lives have nothing to do with their public performance are simply excuses to cover their shame.

Good leadership requires knowledge, character, and principles.

The husbandman must first be partaker of the fruit is the way Scripture states it, which simply means that the leader must first practice what he wants others to do before they follow him.[3]

There can be no effective public denunciation unless there is first a private renunciation.

In 1 Kings 13, the Bible tells of a man of God who was commanded to go preach the Word, but to live a certain way while going and coming.

57

Living his consecration made preaching the Word effective.

Transposition is a common problem in our society. Whether it's a secretary transposing letters, words, or phrases, or a preacher transposing the Word and consecration. Many ministers preach their consecration and try to live the preached Word, instead of living their consecration and preaching the Word.

When ministers try to fit every member of their congregation into their mold, all they do is make moldy Christians.

My wife, Nancy, and I have a wonderful couple as friends and enjoy their company and ministry. Jim and Joy Dawson have done much good in their ministry with Youth for a Mission throughout the world.

Joy had come to teach in the church where I was pastoring many years ago. One morning I had the opportunity to play a round of golf and asked Joy if she wanted us to go along for the walk. She did and came with us.

It was a beautiful, sunny day, an ideal day for recreation. While walking, doing handstands and cartwheels, and jogging occasionally, Joy kept a conversation going with me as I tried to drive, chip, and putt.

As we were coming to the end of the course, Joy said to me gaily, "I think God has something for you and your congregation, Ed."

"What?" I asked.

"Something so important that I must wait until tomorrow and give it to the whole congregation," she replied.

"Give it to me now, then to them tomorrow," I stated as I looked over the putt I was trying to make while carrying on the conversation.

"I don't think so," was her rebuttal.

I stopped, looked at her, paused a moment, thought, then turned back to line up the putt while saying, "If it's so important give it to me now."

Just as I readied to putt she told me what it was.

"God is giving you the opportunity to be one of His few successes or one of his thousands of disappointments. To be one of God's few successes, you need a far higher degree of holiness and a far better understanding of intercession."

I missed the putt, but got the message. It has been part of my life since then.

Taking up—not giving up—is the issue of leadership.

When you accept God's commandments, you agree with Him.

The place of agreement is the place of power.

Joseph was a leader with a servant's heart. His entire life was one of serving others.

You can be one of God's few successes or one of his thousands of disappointments.

Agree with God.

Chapter 8

CONFESSION IS GOOD FOR YOU

Once I was in Vista, California for a series of meetings. The outstanding characteristic of these meetings was the number of Marines who were attending from Camp Pendleton nearby. These marines literally gave themselves to God wholeheartedly and walked out of those meetings with the joy of the Lord, the effervesence of God's presence, and a divine glow radiating from their countenance. They knew God.

One evening one of the men attending seemed reluctant to commit himself to the Lord, so several of his buddies gathered around to encourage him. Taking him off to a side room where there was more privacy, they asked me to join them and lead him in a prayer.

Did I ever. Every element of contrition, repentance, forgiveness, assurance, and praise was in it. There was just one thing missing.

When it came time for him to express his appreciation to the Lord for such saving grace, and thank the Lord for His forgiveness, and praise the

Lord for the work of redemption in his heart, he would not do it.

Months later in conversation with the pastor about the marines and what had been the results in their lives, he told me the only one who had not continued on in Christ was the one who would not consummate his salvation by confession.

The marine's sin was one of omission.

The principle is that you are committed to what you confess.

Joseph confessed his dream.

It was in the confession of that dream that he established his faith and the course of his life.

The confirmation of our faith is established by the confession of our mouth.

Mrs. Cole and I were once hosting a nightly television show. During the course of one of the programs, we began to discuss with our guests the blessedness of the assurance and joy there is in knowing Jesus Christ as Savior and Lord.

The next day a lady called and said she and her husband had an emergency. Could I see them? "Surely," I said. So they drove forty miles to the television station and walked into my office to tell me about their emergency.

Their emergency consisted of the fact that they had seen and heard the program, but did not have the assurance of joy we were talking about.

In the course of trying to help them, I asked them if they believed in God, in Jesus Christ, and in God's Word.

"Yes," they said.

"Have you confessed your sins?" I asked.

"Yes," again came the reply.

"Did God faithfully forgive you and cleanse you of all unrighteousness?" was my question.

"We don't know," they stated.

I looked at them, and they looked at me. I reached for a Bible, opened it, and began reading. When I finished reading, I asked them again if God had forgiven them.

Again their answer was the same, "We don't know."

"Your problem is very simple," I said.

They smiled at each other and turned to me for their solution. The solution was in the two words I gave them.

"You're unbelievers!"

The shock was electric.

I hastened to show them from the Word that "If we confess our sins, he (God) is faithful and just to forgive us our sins, and to cleanse us from all unrighteousness."[1]

"Did you confess your sins?" I asked them.

"Yes."

"Did God forgive you?" I pressed.

Suddenly, with dawning recognition, they incredulously asked me, "You mean all we have to do is take God at His Word?"

That's it.

Simply take God at His Word.

You can't do God's part; God will not do yours.

Simply take God at His Word.

You can't do God's part; God will not do yours.

Confession must be balanced. Repentance must be balanced by faith. Believing must be balanced by receiving. Tenderness must be balanced by toughness.

Balance is the key to life.

Scripture teaches us to confess out our sin, and then confess in our righteousness. What you believe is what you confess. To confess and not believe the confession is hypocrisy.

Words are the expression of our life.

Jesus Christ came as the "Word" incarnate, the express image of God. Jesus is the expression of God on earth.

All God's creative power is in His Word.

Scripture says that God upholds all things by the word of His power.[2]

Life is composed of your choices and constructed by your words.

We are the sum total of all the words we have ever spoken, or those spoken to us which we have received into our lives.

My whole life and ministry today has been constructed by words and is being presently upheld by them.

Words written in the Constitution of the

United States upheld a nation during the Watergate crisis.

Words spoken each Sunday from the pulpit uphold the congregation in a local church week by week.

Words both written and spoken uphold large universities with instruction.

Every word spoken has creative power.

Words will create in the positive or negative. They will build up or tear down.

In February of 1980, while on my way to a men's retreat in Oregon, the Holy Spirit inspired a command for the men in my heart and mind. It was just one sentence, but it changed my life.

The response from that "word" was so phenomenal, I began almost immediately to conduct rallies and seminars for *men only* in all the major cities of the United States.

In May of that year, while speaking at a conference in Pittsburgh, I paused, looked at the congregation, and said, "Pray for me that God will release me to a national ministry to men."

In September of that year, kneeling in a rustic cabin at Hume Lake, California, the Lord again impressed me to "major in ministry to men."

In November, while at an intercessory prayer meeting, someone prayed that God would give ten thousand men in attendance at our rallies in 1981. That was received as the will of God, acted upon, and that year over 15,000 men attended.

But it was April 24, 1981, when George Otis said, "This ministry is running late," that the break occurred in my life.

Within twenty-four hours, I had resigned every attachment or engagement. On Sunday, I walked into the church where I was pastoring and told them, "This may be the most unique service you are ever in because when I pray the benediction it will be my last time here as Pastor."

With the benediction, Mrs. Cole and I left a stunned congregation and launched this ministry to men.

Today as I type this manuscript it is just weeks since we had our National Christian Men's Event with 7,800 *men only* in attendance. One of the largest meetings of it's kind in contemporary church history.

All of it constructed by words that God, others, or myself had spoken. The entire ministry with thousands of men now involved is upheld by the words written and spoken.

It is God's pattern.

God spoke, and His Word went forth to produce what His Word commanded.

My purpose in telling you this is to make sure that you understand that God-given dreams, and the confessing of them, is still the process God uses today to accomplish his purposes.

God did it for Joseph.

God did it for me.

God will do it for you.

Confess your own God-given dream.

Put yourself into it and make it become a reality.

Do it.

Chapter 9

IT'S IN YOUR MOUTH

One of the things that amazes me is the number of hypocrites in the world. I don't mean the ones who talk about the Lord but then don't live what they say. I'm talking about the ones who refuse to talk about or live what they really know in their heart.

Hypocrisy is the sin that walks silent, except to God. "Part actor," one who plays a part, is the definition of the word hypocrisy.

In stage plays years ago, an actor changed character by using a mask. The mask was a disguise. Today that is carried over into our lives as one who is a hypocrite. A "mask-wearer."

Generally speaking, it applies to a person who says one thing with his mouth then lives in another manner entirely. Or one who believes one thing in his heart, but says another with his mouth.

Phil would talk with me about the things of God when we were together; but when I would meet him when he was with other people, he wouldn't do it. Peer pressure, fear of man, moral cowardice, and other motives restrain people from identifying with Jesus.

I'll never forget the day I was on an airplane talking to my neighboring passenger. He was a chemical engineer working with an oil company in the fields of California. Every other word he used was a profanity.

His roustabout days in the field must have carried over to these more sedate times. Great guy, but, man, could he swear. He talked about God and Jesus all the time, not in praise, but in damnation. My spirit was really being grieved with it all.

All the talking was accompanied by an equal amount of liquor. It seemed loquaciousness poured out of the liquor.

Finally, when he paused to get a breath, he asked me what I did for a living. "I'm a minister," was all I said. The cigarette went out, the bottle got tucked away, and the profanity left as he began to tell me of his membership in a church in California, his involvement with a youth organization, and what great good his fraternal organization was doing for humanity.

His mask changed.

I looked at him and wondered how many masks he wears. One for his wife, another for his children, boss, fellow employees, fraternity brothers, neighbors, and God only knows how many more.

He's the kind of guy I'm talking about.

The kind who down in his heart believes

that Christ is his Savior, but won't confess it or live it. They don't confess it because they don't want to have to live it. These also accuse the Church of having so many hypocrites. Hogwash.

You're committed to what you confess.

The reason so many today do not want to recite marriage vows is because they don't want to make any commitment. "Till death do us part" requires too much giving to make it a reality.

You know a marriage has serious problems when either party stops confessing their love. Or says it, but doesn't believe it. Hypocritical.

I was speaking at a church in the Northwest part of our continent and had just finished giving the principle that we "are committed to what we confess." As I said that, the Spirit of God welled up in my soul, and I looked out over that audience of fifteen hundred people with a "word" from God.

"I don't know where you are, Sir, but you're here tonight somewhere. You have never confessed Jesus Christ as your Savior on the job, and the reason you haven't is because you have not wanted to commit yourself to living the life of Jesus in front of other men," I charged.

"You, Sir, are a moral coward, and I command you in the name of Jesus Christ of Nazareth to repent. Ask God to forgive you of that sin, confess Jesus Christ publicly tonight, and tomorrow when you go to work, know that you will confess Him on the job and be willing to commit yourself to living the lifestyle of Jesus in front of other men.''

It was a powerful moment, and it went through that group of people like an electric shock. But I pressed the point home.

''Wherever you are, Sir, get out of your seat and come down here and openly admit Jesus Christ is your Savior and Lord. Now!''

Men all over that audience jumped to their feet and began to run to the front of the building. Those men reacted like men. It was a startling sight to see. Women were standing in the back of the building clapping their hands at the sight of those men making such an open declaration to the glory of God.

Many of them enjoyed a freedom, a liberty, and a new dimension of manhood never experienced before .

Confession has the potential to do good or harm.

Jephthah made a rash vow concerning his daughter, and, rather than recant, repent, or admit it was a hasty vow, he kept it, causing her pain and him sorrow.[1]

King Herod did the same with John the Baptist. The commitment to his confession that he would give up half his kingdom caused him to behead John the Baptist even though he was sorry about it.[2]

Many miss receiving from God through a sense of unworthiness or inferiority.

"No good thing will he withhold from them that walk uprightly."[3]

Joseph received all that God gave him. A dream, favor, wisdom, and prosperity.

Receiving and confessing is as important as believing.

If, after all the believing, you cannot receive and tell others, all the believing is nullified.

Joseph didn't create the dream, God did. He just received it when God gave it.

God is the Creator.

God created man in His image and for His glory. In so doing man received something by creation that neither the animal, vegetable, or mineral kingdoms have.

Creative power.

The Bible says, "God spoke," and it was done. What His Word said, His Spirit brought into being.

It is only through the worthiness of Jesus Christ who purchased God's riches of grace for men that we receive anything from God. That is why it is always by faith, always a gift, always freely given.

Nothing we do can earn anything from God. Our whole relationship with God is based on trust.

Al and I were talking one day about faith, trust, love, and how we must all learn that receiving is as important as believing. Drawing from his football days, both when he played and as a spectator, he grinned at me and said, "Hey, you know those guys who are All-American receivers on the football teams? Well I'm an All-American receiver on God's team."

Trust God for your needs.

Believe God for great things.

And then receive great things from God.

Chapter 10

MASTER YOUR PASSION

Master your passion or your passion will master you.

Joseph learned this principle in his experience with Potiphar's wife. He learned what many other single men have had to learn—how to control their passions.

Everyone has a master passion.

With some it's power, with others it's sex, and with still others it's pleasure, or it's a variety of things. It was Joseph's God-consciousness, his identification with God, his character of Christlikeness, that enabled him to resist the temptation and glorify God.

Joseph developed his character in the aloneness that he had with God as a shepherd boy during the days and nights that he tended his father's flocks.

Decisions made on the spur of the moment really come out of the development of a character over a long period of time. The truth is the decisions we make are rooted and grounded in our character.

You really don't make a decision for or against righteousness in a moment of temptation. You really make that decision prior to that time when you have let the Holy Spirit quicken the Word of God to you, and in those hours you developed a God-consciousness and Christlikeness.

Consequently, when times of crisis come, your decisions that are rooted and grounded in your character will give honor to God.

The criteria of holiness is the honor of God.

In counseling with people over the last several decades, I've never met anyone who committed adultery or fornication on a spur-of-the-moment decision that had not had previous impure thoughts, desires, and appetites. Their decision may have been on the spur of the moment, but the desire had been in their spirit for a long time.

Generally the sin of omission where they had not prayed, obeyed, or meditated on God's Word did not allow the character of Christlikeness to come forth in their lives in those times of temptation.

Decision always translates into energy. Until you make the decision, you don't have the energy to do anything. But once you make the decision, you're supplied with the energy to do that very thing.

The test of true character is not what you do in public, but what you think about when you're all alone. Where does your mind go? Where is your heart's affection? That's where your character is really revealed.

What are your meditations, fantasies, and dreams?

The only person that can know that, other than God, is you. Who are you and what are you by yourself? What is it that pleases you and your thought processes? What is it? That's where your real character is.

Potiphar's wife had the "spirit of the spoiler." The spirit of the spoiler is a satanic spirit and spoils everything it touches. It's a marauder of men's morals, a despoiler of men's spirits, and a contaminating, polluting activity.

There isn't anything that Satan does not spoil. What he wants, of course, is to take the place of God. That messianic ambition in him has never changed. It tried to spoil heaven; did spoil Eden; and is spoiling men's lives to this day. It is that spirit in the world, in the lives of others, that will attempt to seduce you. Scripture says that when we are drawn away by our lusts, sin can exist and bring forth death.[1]

Potiphar's wife had the "spirit of the spoiler."

The spirit of the spoiler in Potiphar's wife wanted Joseph. She desired him. She coveted him.

She was greedy for him. She wanted to possess him.

The only way she knew how do that was through the act of sex. To have sex with him meant that he had succumbed to her beauty, to her power, and to her own kind of authority. Joseph turned her down by simply saying, "No."

But she didn't come once and stop. She kept after him, day after day after day. There was that constant nagging temptation—the constant application of her temptation to his morals.

Temptation is like that. You can say no to it once, but be assured that it will come around again. You may have to battle the same thing over and over again until finally there is ultimate victory.

There was a climactic moment to it all.

Potiphar's wife made herself to become a beautiful, sensuous, and attractive woman. She prepared herself for the moment of contest. She gave the servants the night off, enticed Joseph to her bedroom, made herself available, and simply said, "Lie with me."[2]

Joseph wouldn't do it.

Courage is exemplified, at times, by our ability to turn and run.

Joseph exemplified his courage as a man by running from youthful lust. Fleeing it. When he turned to run, his actions said he didn't want anything to do with her. But she grabbed hold of his tunic and held it in her hand.

She suffered rejection. She vowed for revenge. Her vindictiveness accused Joseph. Her accusation of his attempted rapacious assault was based on the circumstantial evidence of his tunic in her hand.

She based her accusation on a lie. Joseph based his innocence on the truth.

There were three who knew the truth. Potiphar's wife, Joseph, and the Lord.

Truth is not an option in life. It is an absolute.

Truth will always win. Truth can never be defeated. Truth can never die. Truth was crucified, laid in a grave, and rose the third day. The truth that set the pattern and gave the principle to all truth was Jesus Christ.

Potiphar's wife accused Joseph of trying to rape her. Her accusation was based on lies, deceit, and fraud.

The interesting thing about this account is that, when the accusation was made, everyone believed the lie. They knew Joseph's character, honesty, integrity, sincerity. They knew Joseph. They had been blessed and favored because of Joseph's presence in that household.

Yet they believed a lie.

Because people are negative by nature it is easier to believe a lie than it is the truth. That's why we must be converted from the negative to the positive. Even when proven innocent, people often will not believe the innocence.

Joseph had proven to be loyal, honest, and truthful, but the servants believed a lie about him. Joseph had proven to be a blessing to Potiphar and all that he did. But, when Potiphar's wife said, "See, he hath brought in an Hebrew unto us to mock us; he came in unto me to lie with me."[3] Potiphar believed her rather than Joseph—even though he knew the character of both.

In her accusation, Joseph first met the prejudice against his race. The racial, ethnic implication of what she said when she said, "an Hebrew to mock us," showed the Egyptian prejudice toward the Jews.

She distorted what was already there with circumstantial evidence in order to further inflame the passions of prejudice that were running rampant in the hearts of the Egyptians who were already against the Israelites.

Potiphar believed her, rather than believing Joseph.

There is an old saying that "blood is thicker than water."

Potiphar made a wrong decision. It was the same kind of a decision that Adam had made in Eden. Potiphar never asked Joseph the truth. Adam never asked God about Eve's invitation in the garden. The absence of seeking truth and asking God is evident in both of their mistakes.

What grave consequences the sin of omission holds for everyone.

Potiphar's wife was insulted, seething with

rage, and determined to spoil Joseph. He remained silent under the onslaught of his accusers.

Like Jesus who when brought before the Sanhedrin and before the high priest held his peace, Joseph also remained silent. It was said of Jesus that he was "led as a sheep to the slaughter" not unlike Joseph.

The same thing happened in the life of Elijah when he had to face the "spirit of the spoiler" in Jezebel—and Samson with Delilah—and John the Baptist with Herodias.

The battle Joseph fought was when he was all alone with Potiphar's wife. There was no one to sustain, give him counsel or advice, or help him ward off Potiphar's wife. He had to fight that battle alone. His manhood was called into question. The determining factor was what he did when he was all alone with his master passion. It's the same today whether you're a man or a woman. *Joseph fled.*

"How can I do this great wickedness, and sin against God," Joseph said.[4] His identification with God was real and true. He was not concerned about himself but about the honor of God. It was what happened to the testimony of God in his life that was of paramount concern.

Though Potiphar's wife and everyone believed the lie, still truth was Joseph's vindication.

If someone says something is wrong and 50,000 people believe it, if it's wrong in it's origination, then it's wrong no matter how many people may repeat it. Remember the greatest potential in our life is in what we believe. Joseph believed the truth; others believed a lie.

God knew the truth and ultimately vindicated Joseph.

When we retain our integrity in the face of temptation, we will not consumate that temptation and therefore sin against God.

It is no sin to be tempted.

When we retain our integrity in the face of temptation, we will not consummate that temptation and therefore sin.

Sin is conceived when we succumb to the temptation. If we don't submit to it, and we reject it, the devil is going to turn around and accuse us. He will try to make us think that we're guilty, even though we only thought it and were tempted by it.

Let's say that you are a man, and you see an attractive girl coming down the street. All of a sudden, there's a tempting thought that goes through your mind.

When that tempting thought goes through your mind, you simply say, "I am a child of God. I am a son of the Living God. I am the righteousness of God in Christ." You begin to confess positively. You command that thing to get out of your mind, and it's gone! That temptation is gone.

Yet, two blocks down the street, you hear this accusation in your mind like a fiery dart trying to poison your mind saying, "Well, you thought it, therefore you're guilty, because the Bible says if you think it, you're guilty of doing it."

Remember that the devil based his temptation of Eve on a half truth. He'll always try to get you on a half truth.

The Bible doesn't say that if you simply think it, you're guilty of it. It says that if you "think ye evil in your heart."[5] That means if you *meditate* on it, if you *fantasize over* it, if you have a *desire* to do it, if you have an *affection* for it, an *affinity* for it, and you *dwell* on it.

It doesn't say that if that temptation runs through your mind, it says that if you think evil in your heart.

The devil knows that. But he gives you a half truth on the Scripture.

So, if you're tempted and reject it, when the devil says, "Well, you thought it. Therefore you're guilty of it," you have a right to tell him, "Hey, it was your temptation to begin with." Command him in the name of Jesus Christ to take his temptations and accusations and go back to the place he came from.

I don't advocate that you say it exactly that way, but that's what you mean.

Satan has no leverage where there is no sin.

You're not identified with sin when it's been forgiven.

The thought is the father to the deed. Because Joseph had never thought about sinning with Potiphar's wife, he was able to steadfastly resist when tempted.

Tempting thoughts are like fiery darts to the mind and must be quenched with the shield of faith which is the confession of Jesus Christ.

Remember, even if the "spirit of the spoiler" has spoiled your mind or heart, the blood of Jesus Christ can cleanse you entirely and, in the sight of God, leave you without a blemish.

God identifies you with His righteousness, you do the same. Identify yourself with His righteousness, and you will always master the passion.

Joseph did.

You can do the same.

Be a victor, not a victim.

Chapter 11

IS GOD MAD AT YOU?

Nancy and I were hosting a television program. The day after one of our programs, we got a call from a lady in a nearby city. She said her husband was in deep, deep depression and wondered if we would minister to him. We said of course we would.

The following night, she showed up with her husband. He was an extremely successful businessman, a developer of large resorts. Several successive events put him into such severe depression that he would sit in the house with the window shades drawn, darkness all around, isolated in his commiseration and condemnation.

What had happened was that in the development of a very large resort, the funding was withdrawn at the last moment, and the project was placed in jeopardy. Shortly after that, his lovely granddaughter perished in a fire in a garage. Several other such instances made him wonder about his relationship with God. Finally, he convinced himself that because of these circumstances, God was mad at him.

Depression is generally caused by resentment or a sense of loss. In his case, he felt both.

When I saw him at the television station, I took him into my office. We sat down on the couch. I put my arm around his shoulders and began to pray very softly. I didn't try to counsel or do anything other than pray. As I prayed, he began to sob almost uncontrollably. I continued to pray and his sobbing began to cease. He began to enter into the spirit of prayer, intercession, and praise.

After some minutes, it was like a plug had come unstopped in his spirit. He began to thank the Lord for His goodness and grace and favor. The change was as dramatic as in the case of Saul on the road to Damascus. He went home with his wife a changed, buoyant, joyous man.

The truth was that God never was mad at him. It was a lie based on circumstantial evidence in his life. When he finally received the truth of God's love and grace and favor, he was restored in his relationship.

God is our justifier. Satan is our accuser.

God justifies us from every accusation.

However, many people resent God and are mad at Him. They believe that God has favored someone else and been partial to them, or taken a loved one from them, or somehow God is punishing them.

The truth is that, as in the case of Job, Satan

accuses God to men and men to God in order to produce a distance between them. If allowed to remain, that distance can be the same distance between heaven and hell.

In our lives, it is easy at times for us to believe a lie. I had finished ministering after the Sunday morning service and was talking to some of the people and praying with them. I looked into the face of one young lady who was smiling beautifully and asked her, "What happened to you this morning?"

"When I was a young girl," she said, "my mother died. All these years, I have resented God because He took my mother. This morning I asked God to forgive me. And if you really want to know the truth, though I knew He didn't do it, I forgave God. Doesn't that sound strange?"

As I looked at her, I wondered how many others held resentments toward God because of what they wrongfully believed He had done to them in their lives. They believed a lie. Receiving and believing truth changed their life and their relationship with God.

The same kind of a thing happened with a lady whose husband I had known many years before. He had been involved with me in the activities of youth work. Many years later, he had gone off with another woman. He left his wife alone to fend for herself. Living alone in Fullerton, California, working to support herself, she'd come home one evening and been raped at knife point in an elevator.

She blamed God for her husband's leaving, the rape, and the hardness of her life. She resented God because of the life she was living. It was a joy for me to watch her that night as she repented of her resentment toward God and asked God to forgive her. It changed her believing. It changed her life.

Do you resent God? Do you think He is mad at you, or are you mad at Him?

If so, it is keeping you from an intimate relationship with Him. *God is for you not against you.*

The levels of the knowledge of God we live on hold potential for God's goodness to us. The levels are:

God is *for* me.

God is *with* me.

God is *in* me.

The Psalmist said, "God is for me;" Matthew reveals the Name of Jesus as Emmanual, "God is with us;" and in Ephesians Paul writes that "God is in us."

The highest level, of course, is that which knows and understands that by the indwelling of the Holy Spirit, God is at work at all times in us to produce our highest good which is His perfect will.

Jesus said, "Blessed is he, whosoever shall not be offended in me."[1] The Pharisees were offended at Jesus because they saw in Him things they did not like, and He could do no mighty work among them.

Jonah was offended at God because God forgave the sins of Nineveh when they repented and turned to God.[2]

My friend J.P. was once offended with God. When he saw the truth, God was able to bring renewed blessing into his life.

J.P. worked as a salesman in an automobile agency. He was serving God with as much as he could give God, and doing it spiritually, physically, financially and every other way.

He worked alongside another salesman who had no concern for God, church, or goodness. J.P. endured the cigar smoke, profanity, unclean jokes, and occasional cheating for the sake of the gospel, because he hoped someday to minister the life of Christ to his co-worker.

There came a period of time, however, when J.P. could not sell a car, while the other salesman sold everything in sight. J.P. was suffering a financial famine while the salesman next to him was prospering abundantly.

J.P. got mad at God.

This went on for about a month. Then one day, driving across the Oakland Bay Bridge from San Franscisco, J.P. began to pray.

"God, here I am trying to serve You, giving my time, energy, and money to You. I'm being faithful in church with my family and teaching in

Sunday School. Yet here You are blessing this other guy while I suffer. I don't understand You God.

"If this is the way You're going to do things then I might as well quit. You're hurting me and helping him. Why are You blessing him like that and not me?"

By now J.P. was hitting the steering wheel of the car with his hand, talking out loud, and meaning every word of what he was saying. When he had finally prayed himself out and became quiet, J.P. heard a still small voice in his spirit say, *"I'm* not blessing him."

With instant clarity in understanding, J.P. realized that Satan was doing it, not God. The devil was doing it to offend J.P. and make him mad at God. When he saw it, J.P. began to weep. In repentance he asked God to forgive him for his wrong believing. Once again J.P. began to thank God for His goodness and faithfulness.

Back at work, without resentment toward God, financial prospering again began to flow into J.P.'s life.

It was his wrong believing that had been his problem.

When that changed, everything changed.

What you believe about God has the greatest potential for good or harm in your life.

What you believe can attract or repel.

What you believe determines relationships.

What you believe about God will determine

your relationship to Him. What you believe about yourself will determine your relationship with others.

Men like Oral Roberts, Billy Graham, and others have all had sustained ministries because they believe that God is a good God.

God loves you.

When God convicts or convinces us of sin, it's not because He is mad at us but because He loves us. Sin will inhibit and prohibit God's revelation of Himself to us. The purpose of His convicting us of our sins is so that we will confess them out of our lives. Then He can forgive us and reveal Himself to us in greater intimacy.

Many people believe that God is their adversary based on their guilt or condemnation of what their sin is, has been, or was thought to be.

Joseph believed that God was a good God, that God loved him and was working in his behalf. Joseph based his trust of God in his belief in God.

Believe God's Word.

God is not mad at you.

Don't be mad at Him either.

God has revealed Himself as desiring to give you the Kingdom. He's trying now to convince you of it by giving you this word.

Receive it.

Chapter 12

WHEN THE INNOCENT SUFFER

Joseph was persecuted for righteousness' sake.

When he was in jail, he suffered as the guilty, although he was innocent. He was accused, judged, and sentenced as guilty on the basis of circumstantial evidence.

He knew he was innocent. Potiphar's wife knew he was innocent. God knew he was innocent. Yet he was suffering as guilty.

In most prisons, almost universally, men declare their innocence. If not actual innocence, then they accuse society of being partial and unjust in the judicial process toward them.

It's one thing to suffer as guilty when you are guilty; it's another to suffer as guilty when you're innocent.

Next to actual rejection, the most difficult thing for men to suffer is being treated as guilty when they are innocent.

Yet the principle of the cross of Christ is that the innocent do suffer for the guilty.

It's found in every area of life.

Insurance premiums are high for those who do not drink because of the loss incurred by those who do. Liberties of the law-abiding citizen are restricted because of the activities of the lawless.

We live in a perverted society.

That is why we need God to change it all back for us.

Some years ago Ed accepted a position with an East Coast company. When he arrived, his delight with his new-found position was only short lived, for within weeks he found things that dismayed and distressed him.

It seemed that the previous administration and executives in it had committed things that were either immoral, illegal, or unethical. As a result, when Ed took his new position, all the previous misdeeds with their resultant problems became his. He began to suffer the penalties of his predecessors' errors and mistakes.

Ed had to suffer the indignities that rightfully should have gone to others.

He developed deep-seated resentments which eventually became real hostility. No matter how he struggled, he seemed only to get deeper and deeper into the morass of problems.

There was a real sense of betrayal on Ed's part toward those who had enmeshed him in it and had never advised him of it before he got into it. He felt outrage. Umbrage.

The punishment that should have gone to

others who were guilty was instead being heaped on him.

In the throes of it all, Ed was driving along the highway, feeling sorry for himself, and expressing his resentment toward others to God.

"Lord, why do I have to suffer the guilt of those who were guilty, when I'm innocent. I didn't do anything wrong, yet I'm suffering for it. It just isn't right!"

He was telling God exactly how he felt. But then, that is reality. God understands every emotion, attitude, and motive of the heart. Why try to pontificate in prayer with God?

As he drove down the road enumerating the sins of others, sympathizing with himself in his misery, and crying out to God about what he felt was an injustice being done him, God did a beautiful thing for him.

God showed him a cross.

When Ed saw in his spirit the cross where Christ died, he then realized the innocent do suffer for the guilty.

When he saw that Jesus Christ had taken upon Himself all the sin, wretchedness, rejection, betrayal, grossness, coarseness, and rebellion, he broke down and cried, "God forgive me."

In that moment all the bitterness, resentment, outrage, umbrage, anger, frustration, everything he had been feeling went completely, totally out of his spirit.

Like the work of the Holy Spirit in regeneration, it took but a moment for the change to take place. At that particular moment, Ed realized that Jesus bore it all and did it all for him.

Instead of acting like an unmerciful servant by judging others, blaming them, and reproaching them, he suddenly realized how much God had forgiven him. With that realization, humility took the place of pride, submission took the place of rebellion, and love took the place of fear.

An appreciation, compassion, desire to help, benefit, and bless those involved took the place of the negatives. The cross changed his whole attitude.

Jesus took it all.

Remember this the next time you begin to be resentful toward someone else because you suffer for their guilt. Give it all to Jesus Christ, and let Him give you His grace, love, and forgiveness.

I watched this happen one night at a men's retreat outside of Colorado Springs. During the course of the evening there had been the teaching of the principle of "Release," followed by a time of prayer.

As the men began to share with everyone what was happening in their lives, one man astounded us all with what he had to say.

"Until tonight I never understood what was wrong with my life. For seven years I've wanted to live for God, but I've lived on a roller coaster. One day forgiven, the next day sinning and needing to be forgiven again. One day guilty, the next innocent, only to become guilty again. I could never seem to get my act together for any sustained period of time.

"Tonight God changed my life. I want to thank God for that.

"You see, my father's reputation in the town where we lived was so bad that people hated me simply because I was his son. I had to bear the sins of my dad. I grew up rejected, isolated, ridiculed, and persecuted because of who my dad was. I had to fight to survive. I hated my dad. I hated him so much that on the day of his funeral, while he was lying in a casket, I spit in his face.

"And, I knew who my mother was, but I never met her until I was sixteen. It was my best friend who introduced me. He had been telling me for some time about an older woman he was going with, and how she gave him all the sex he wanted, and what she was like. When he brought her around to meet me, I realized she was my mother. I hated her for what she was.

"It never dawned on me until tonight that because of my unforgiveness of my mom and dad, I was retaining their sins in my life and making the same mistakes and committing the sins they did.

"Tonight, by the help of the Holy Spirit, I forgave them both and released their sins out of my life. For the first time in my life, I feel free."

He had been suffering as guilty, though innocent. It happens. That's the reason Jesus Christ came to make it possible for us not only to be forgiven, but to forgive and be released from the sins of all men.

There is real freedom for all of us.

God's transcendent glory is for all of us.

Joseph described it best when he said to his brothers who had sought to kill him, sold him down the river, never understood him, always suspected him, and could never receive his love: *"But as for you, you thought evil against me; but God meant it for good."*[1]

But God.

Those two words are the turning point for all human life.

Because of them your whole life can change.

Whatever you are going through in your life right now can be changed. Persecution, tribulation, suffering as guilty though innocent—there is an answer, there is a cross, there is His transcendent glory.

But God.

Put those two words on your wall, your dashboard, your mirror in your bathroom and your refrigerator. Put them in bold lettering so you can see night and day that God is at work in you to produce your highest good. He is a good God.

If you're going through something right now that's hard for you to take, just say those two words. Say them over and over and over again.

Let me tell you about a friend. He is the pastor of a large, successful church. To all outward appearances, he is a man who is enjoying the best of everything in life. He's my brother and my friend. When I went to that city to hold a large "men only" rally, he met me at the airport to drive me to a radio station. We had exchanged some small talk before he unloaded on me.

"Ed, I don't know what I'm going to do. I'm at the end of my rope. I feel like I've got to declare bankruptcy. I don't want to, but it seems like that's the only thing I can do. I'm fifteen thousand dollars in debt. My wife has to clean houses for a living, and my times of seeking God are constantly beset by thoughts of my financial distress.

"A year ago I was solvent. Now this year I am deeply in debt and feel as though I am in financial bondage, and I don't know what to do."

He continued to tell me some of the details of his problem and the pressure he was under. As he talked, I prayed. I knew he was going to ask me for some kind of help or advice, and I wanted to be able to give it in order to help him. Not just assuage his feelings.

That's the difference between the gospel's message and men's abilities to counsel. The gospel is good news, but men generally only give good advice. Ministers who preach good advice but don't have the good news will not change lives and convert souls.

When he finished talking to me, I looked at him and asked, "Tell me about your elder's board of deacons or whatever it is."

He said he had five men on the board, and I asked him what they were like.

He told me that two of them were excellent men who were self-employed businessmen, full of faith and vision for the work of God. Two others were good men, but at times they had to be persuaded to advance the cause of Christ. When it came to the fifth, he said, "He's a good man, but so negative. He's always sick, has no job, and has lost his car. The only time we ever took a special offering in our church was to help buy him a car."

I looked at him with dawning recognition of the problem and with a revelation that could only come from the Spirit of God.

"Bill," I cried, "That man is not negative or conservative. He's covetous. His covetousness is his sin. He's living under the curse because of his sin. He's not under the blessing. And what you have done is to accept his economic philosophy into your life. By doing so you have accepted his spirit of covetousness into your finances. He's brought the curse upon you and upon your church. Probably in every other area of life, you're blessed except that one. The reason for that is you have become a partaker of another man's sin."

He looked at me with amazement. He saw it.

"What will I do?"

"What you've got to do is ask God to forgive you for being a partaker of another man's sin. You are the innocent suffering for the guilty. But you're doing it in a negative and not a positive way. You're suffering the curse instead of the blessing, and you must get it out of your life. Once having been forgiven, you must go to him and tell him about it, and then from there you've got to tell your wife and ask God to change your life."

He went to his wife and told her what had happened. One Sunday morning before his congregation, he broke down and with great humility shared it with them. They responded in a positive, warm, and affectionate way, and it blessed him. He went to that member of his board, reproved him, and told him he had to change or leave the board. Within thirty days Bill had a large increase in his salary, the members of the Christian school had all received a healthy raise, and the level of contributions and gifts to the church had increased. God had done a miracle.

Everything in life has the potential for good or harm. That's even true when the innocent suffer for the guilty. To suffer in innocence for the guilt of another, in order to see their lives benefited, is positive. To do it and suffer as Jim did is negative. God can change your negatives to positives.

Put your faith in God, in His Word, and in His abilities.

Chapter 13

SET A PRIORITY OR TWO

Joseph never knew life without pressure.

Pressure has existed since Adam was expelled from Eden. The reason why the events in Joseph's life loom as large as they do is because of the pressure under which he lived.

Pressure always magnifies.

Recently, we held a "National Christian Men's Event." Over seven thousand men poured in from Honolulu, Miami, Boston, Los Angeles, and New York. Men literally spent hundreds of dollars to attend a meeting that began at 9:00 in the morning and ended at 6:00 that evening. Nine hours. That's all it was.

The day before the meeting, I gathered the staff around me and gave them the principle that *pressure always magnifies.*

I told them because we had condensed, compacted, and compressed the time, everything that would be said and done would be magnified out of all proportion to anything else they had ever been involved in.

I used an illustration concerning Reggie Jackson, the baseball player. If he were to hit a homerun in May, during a ball game in Milwaukee, it would merit small type on the back page of the sports section of the daily newspaper. But when he hit it in the sixth inning of the seventh game of the World Series, it was on the front page all over the world. The difference was the pressure.

The difference in men who succeed and fail is in their ability to handle pressure.

Men who drove covered wagons across the United States of America to open up, explore, and settle the west knew what pressure was. They had to contend with the dangerous situation of dealing with those who felt their land was being stolen. How they handled it and how they reacted to it made the difference in them and their wagon trains.

The same for those who explored this world. Colombus, Magellan, Admiral Perry, and even the modern-day Cousteau knew pressure.

There are different kinds of pressure.

Jesus knew the ultimate pressure. He faced it, overcame it, and rose triumphant over it all. Therefore, whoever believes in Him and receives His Spirit can live the same way.

But men who become heroes and accomplish great things are not only able to handle pressure, but also have a value system in which their priorities are set aright.

Traveling throughout much of this world I

have seen the monuments, statues, markers, and plaques that have been erected to men who have been leaders of revolutions, liberation movements, and have led their countries in war and peace.

These are men who laid down their lives for causes in which they firmly believed.

I vividly recall the woman who walked through Golden Gate Park and died under a rapist's attack rather than surrender her virtue. Rows of white crosses in our nation's military cemetery mark the graves of men who have given up their lives for the freedom of democracy that America enjoys today.

There is a principle that says *some things in life are more important than life itself.*

John the Baptist, rather than compromise truth, was beheaded. James chose to speak of the glory of God and the revelation of Jesus Christ to those who had crucified Christ rather than remain silent. Steven was stoned to death for his stand.

Jesus gave us that principle when He gave His life for our salvation. "God so loved the world, that He gave His only begotten Son, that whosoever believeth in Him should not perish, but have everlasting life."[1]

Even Esau knew that. He sold his birthright for a mess of pottage.[2] Remember, this principle has the potential for both good or harm. In Esau's case it was harm.

There are some people who feel that a cigarette, a bottle of beer, a night of sex, or obtaining prestige and power are more important than life itself. They're willing to trade their birthright for moments of pleasure, their marriages for money, and their children for entertainment.

Or what about Eli? His children made themselves evil, and Eli didn't restrain them. When he finally rebuked his children, they didn't pay any attention to him. Eli ultimately lost his life and ministry because he pandered and spoiled his children at the expense of the Word of God.

Eli's posterity was cut off because he spoiled his children at the expense of the will of God. God considered that Eli despised his ministry because of the way he allowed his children to conduct themselves.[3]

Scripture recounts the man named Jairus, a ruler of the synagogue whose daughter was sick. Jairus laid aside his position, power, prestige, and pride in order to come to Jesus and beseech the Lord to heal his daughter. Jairus counted that his daughter's health was worth more than all he had attained in this life. He was willing to surrender it all for the one overriding concern of life—the healing of his daughter. That was worth more than life itself to him.[4]

I was in Alaska ministering in a retreat to men only. A young businessman came up to ask for prayer. His wife was sick with cancer and had been for some time. She had had one leg amputated along with other surgery, and now doctors had told her she had a limited time to live. She had gone to visit her parents and from there to attend a Bible school hoping to receive enough faith in Christ to be healed of her cancer.

During all of this, he had a recurring dream. In his dream he was walking across a field and suddenly saw his wife lying at the base of a tree with a large black cloud coming toward her. He knew it was death. Each time the cloud would come, it grieved him and his dream would end in despair because he didn't know what to do.

Relating the situation to me, he then asked if it made sense.

"Yes," I said. "What you need to do is realize that you've done all you can do. You cannot continue to suffer the guilt of your inability to heal or to provide healing for her. Everything that you could possibly do, you have done. What you need to do now, by faith, is to commit her and her life to the Lord Jesus Christ. Then you can be rid of your guilt and anxiety, and you and your wife can pray and love each other in total release of spirit.

"You need to go to her, tell her you love her, that she's been God's gift to you, and that no matter what happens you're grateful for your thirteen years of marriage, two children, and the years of intimate relationship."

He went off into the woods that afternoon to pray down by the creek at the base of Mount Whitney. Later that afternoon, I saw him walking toward me with a spring in his step, a wave of his hand, and a smile on his face. When he walked up to me, he was a happy man.

"I did it," he said, "I did it. I released her in faith. And while I was out walking in the woods just now, I sat down by a tree and dozed off for a little while. While I was asleep, I had that same recurring dream again.

"Once again in the dream I saw my wife lying at the base of a tree and this big black cloud coming toward her. Before I had been frustrated and despairing, but this time my dream continued. In it I ran over, picked her up and took her to where there was a white cloud. I knew it was the presence of the Lord. When I turned toward the Lord to commit her to Jesus, the black cloud was gone. I want you to know that death has no more fear. No matter what happens, she's the Lord's, and I'm the Lord's."

His faith in Jesus had become more important than his wife's healing.

Some things in life really are more important than life itself.

Chapter 14

ARE YOU READY TO PROSPER?

"And the Lord was with Joseph, and he was a prosperous man."[1]

I want to talk to you about money.

I know that the Word says that real life and real living are not related to how rich we are.

But there are three basic problem areas in relationships. It used to be these were only in the bonds of marriage, but not today.

Those three are: money, sex, and communication.

The use of money is a visible expression of faith. What a man does with his money shows what he does with his life and how much value he places in it.

Money is the closest thing to omnipotence most of us will ever have. With it we can buy power, land, or human bodies.

Some things it cannot buy.

We can buy sex, but we can't buy love. We can buy someone's time, but not their loyalty. We can purchase pleasure, but not happiness.

Remember what we believe will attract or repel.

What you believe about money will attract it or repel it.

The image you have of money determines what you believe about it.

Money is amoral. We give it morality or immorality.

Money is not all there is to tithing. Tithing is not all there is to stewardship. Time, talent, and treasury are involved.

Tithing your time to God can change the world. When David Wilkerson began to tithe his time to God, God gave him the dream that was to become "Teen Challenge." It was during that "tithe-time" that he wrote the "Cross and the Switchblade."

Tithing your talent to the work of God would advance the cause of Christ the way laser light surpasses sound waves.

There are really only three reasons a man doesn't tithe his money—unbelief, fear, or covetousness.

There are only three reasons ministers won't preach about it—unbelief, fear, or pride.

Giving is a release to the spirit.

Giving is an expression of love.

You only know the depth of loving by the degree of giving.

Offerings in the church are not for the health of the preacher, but for the health of the congregation. Occasions for giving are opportunities to prosper. Since I have been closely associated with men these last few years, with their lives, loves, and lusts, I have discovered that many of them have a perverted view of the purpose of prospering. Preachers with personal prejudices convey wrong images.

God's purpose in prospering His people is not for them to gain, but to have enough to give more and more to the work of the Lord.

The purpose is giving—not getting.

Money has the potential of blessing and cursing. Joseph used it to bless humanity.

Money is only a means. Not an end.

When men make it the end of their efforts rather than using it to achieve good, they corrupt it. It's the *lust* of money that is the root of all evil. Love desires to give, lust desires to get.

While in Tulsa something occurred that has stayed with me from then until now. Pastor Billy Joe Daugherty was the catalyst.

During the morning I had been teaching on the subject of "Maximized Manhood." In the course of it, I began to give some principles of the Kingdom of God.

"Jesus taught us that if we love Him, we will obey Him, and if we obey Him, He will manifest Himself to us," I was teaching. "That means *obedience is the evidence of love,* and *manifestation is based on obedience.* A ton of prayer will never produce what an ounce of obedience will.

"One of God's principles," I went on, "is that to 'obey is better than sacrifice.'[2] The reason for that is that *we cannot compensate by sacrifice what we lose through disobedience.*"

There was more, but that much was what was mentioned that night prior to the offering time.

"Folks, I saw something this morning that I never saw before," Pastor Daugherty told his congregation. "The reason some of you are not prospering financially is because you are not sowing the seed. Instead of giving to the work of the Lord, you are sacrificing by prayer and expecting to reap a harvest.

"You cannot compensate by sacrifice what you lose through disobedience. Manifestation is based on obedience. You reap what you sow. These are all Kingdom principles that Dr. Cole has been sharing with us.

"This morning as I listened to those principles the Spirit of God revealed something to me. What I saw was that some of you are having financial problems. The reason you are is because you're not giving to the work of God. Instead of tithing, you are trying to sacrifice by prayer what you're losing through disobedience. Your refusal to tithe is really an act of disobedience. But you heard that to obey is better than sacrifice, and you cannot compensate by sacrifice what you lose through disobedience.

"Some of you need to change. Instead of

trying to work up enough faith to believe God for financial prosperity, you need to start tithing," he finished.

Right on!

The principle is, "Give, and it shall be given unto you."[3]

An offering and an altar call are synonymous. Having once responded to an altar call and given your life to God, you do not do that every service thereafter. From that time forward, you simply put your life in the offering plate.

Sure you do.

During the week you give your time, talent, energy, abilities, emotions, knowledge, and all else you possess where you work. In exchange, you receive money. That money represents your life. What you do with it and how you use it shows what you do with your life.

Jack was having problems with his wife. He had made a large profit, bought a new building, drove an expensive car, but his business began to decrease. Things were really financially very tight, and he needed help.

His wife had been raised to think that poverty and spirituality were synonomous. Therefore it was hard for her to live in prosperity. When he had bought his expensive new car, it was three days before she could get in it, and three years before she wasn't ashamed of it.

The image had been stamped on her mind by parents, pastors, and environment. It was wrong, but she wouldn't change. Actually she thought if she was rich she would not get to heaven.

It's hard for rich people to get to heaven; not because they are rich, but because they trust in their riches.

Poverty is a bondage. There is only glory in it if it is taken as a vow to the Lord. Otherwise there is none.

I know.

For years I had a poverty attitude that made life hard for my wife and children. In those early years of ministry, I really thought that when you "give," "lose," "surrender," it meant never getting anything back.

Thank God for the day He taught me that it isn't giving to lose, but giving to gain that is the principle of the Kingdom.

Today I ride both coach or first class on an airplane, ride in Escorts or Mercedes, stay at Motel 6 or the Kahala Hilton, eat soy beans or pistachio nuts.

Mrs. Cole and our two daughters were once cramped into a two-bedroom apartment. Talk about tension, that can create it.

We prayed and asked the Lord for a larger place to live. He found us one in the nicest neighborhood of our town. The house was perfect for us. But I had a hard time receiving it because of my childhood poverty attitude that was being carried into my later life.

While walking the beach and asking the Lord about it, a very wonderful and beautiful experience occurred.

"Therefore to him that knoweth to do good, and doeth it not, to him it is sin."[4]

I heard the voice of the Lord in my spirit say, "If I asked you to move into a one-bedroom apartment, would you do it?"

"Yes Lord," was my immediate answer.

"Then why won't you move into a three-bedroom house if I ask you to?" I heard Him ask.

Bingo.

The issue wasn't one bedroom or three. The issue was obedience. If God wanted me to prosper by living in a three-bedroom house, and I didn't do it, I would be in sin just as much as not moving into a one-bedroom apartment when He wanted me to.

Since then, where I live has not been a problem.

Is it for you?

God's desire to prosper you isn't for your glory, but for the benefit of His Kingdom.

The issue isn't being rich or poor, but being obedient.

As with everything else, money only has potential.

A Jewish family moved to a town in Germany from their home and took up a whole new cultural way of life. Because he was Jewish, the father could not seem to make his business prosper. Things were going from bad to worse. Finally one day the father came home, gathered his family around him, and announced they were converting from Judaism to Lutheranism. He thought if they would become Lutheran, then their business would prosper.

This so affected the Jewish man's son that as the boy grew up he developed a philosophy about religion. He believed it was the "opiate of the people."

That boy was Karl Marx the founder of Communism.

To this day the world still suffers from the action of one man—Karl Marx's father.

Money is at the root of the communist system.

It's the root problem for more than that.

Hosea is an Old Testament prophet who was married to an unfaithful wife. She loved for hire. She prostituted herself for what her lovers would give her. Prostitution is loving for hire.

Loving God only for material prosperity is a form of spiritual prostitution.

However, it is in the nature of God to give, because it's the manifestation of love.

It is God's nature to prosper us.

But to love Him only for material prosperity is a form of loving for hire.

God used Hosea's wife to show Israel their own sin.

Though our love for God is not to be based

on material prosperity, yet to deny God's right to prosper you materially through unbelief is to deny God's right of Lordship to your life.

Jesus never cursed a fig tree because it bore too much fruit and some spoiled. He only cursed it when it was barren and did not produce anything.

God wants you to prosper in every dimension of your lfie.

Are you ready to prosper?

Do you need to?

Then—prosper.

Chapter 15

GUILT? WHO NEEDS IT!

"And when Joseph's brethren saw that their father was dead, they said, Joseph will peradventure hate us, and will certainly requite us all the evil we did unto him."[1]

With fear in their hearts as to what Joseph would do to them, his brothers sent Joseph a message reminding him what their father had said.

"So shall you say unto Joseph, Forgive, I pray thee now, the trespass of thy brethren, and their sin; for they did unto thee evil: and now, we pray thee, forgive the trespass of the servants of the God of thy father."[2]

Joseph wept when they spoke to him.

As his brothers asked for forgiveness, they fell down before Joseph offering themselves as servants to him.

"And Joseph said unto them, Fear not: for am I in the place of God?"[3]

Joseph comforted them. He imparted cheer, hope, and strength as he spoke kindly to their hearts.

Isn't it interesting that, after all those years, Joseph's brothers retained their sense of guilt.

They felt that Jacob was the restraining influence to Joseph. As long as Jacob was alive, Joseph wouldn't do anything to them. But now, retribution would come to them from Joseph because that restraining influence had been taken away.

They were afraid Joseph would wreck havoc with their lives.

Three immediate results of sin shown to us in the garden when Adam and Eve sinned were guilt, fear, and hiding.

Guilt produced the fear that produced the hiding. Guilt was the result of sin.

Consequently, there was an image created in his brother's minds concerning Joseph that someday, somehow, someplace, ultimately, Joseph was going to get even with them. Joseph was going to requite their sin of them.

They could not conceive that Joseph loved them, that he forgave them with an unconditional forgiveness and love, and that all he would do was to continue to bless them and give them his favor and goodness.

They created an image in their minds of an unforgiving brother.

They could not release the guilt until they asked forgiveness of Joseph.

It's the same way with us and God. You cannot get the guilt out of your life until you ask

God to forgive you. Once God has forgiven you, then you need to forgive yourself.

When we confess our sins, God forgives us. God doesn't hold them against us anymore.

One of the common fallacies that I've heard is if you really forgive, you would forget. The truth is that when you forgive, you don't necessarily forget. You retain the image of that thing in your mind.

By the help of God Himself, through the presence of His Holy Spirit in your life, you can forgive others as God forgives you. You may retain the memory, but you'll never hold it against anyone anymore. You don't retain the pain. You don't retain the sorrow. You don't retain the hurt. You don't retain the regret. You don't retain the desire for vengeance or vindication. You just release it. You may have the memory of it, but the hurt is released.

That's the way Joseph was. Joseph forgave his brothers. The only thing he wanted to do was to benefit, bless, and take care of them.

But because they had never been able to forgive themselves, because they had never asked for forgiveness and received forgiveness to release the guilt, it cropped up again.

Joseph said, paraphrased, "You don't understand. I'm leaving all that up to God. A long time ago I gave all that to God. As far as I'm concerned, you may have meant it to me for evil, but I took it and committed it to God. By God's transcendent glory, He turned it around and made it work for my good. You meant it to me for evil, but God meant it to me for good."

What he experienced wasn't necessarily good. But God made it work for his good, and ultimately it was good for him.

What about your own life? Is there someone that you haven't been able to forgive as God forgives?

Guilt is deadly. Guilt will kill relationships.

I know people that have done something to me, said something about me, or borrowed and never repaid; because of their guilt, they don't want to face me again.

A long time ago, I released that. I learned if anyone owes me money or has cheated me out of money, I don't try to collect from them. I take that missing money to God, and I sow that as seed faith in the Kingdom of God. I say, "Lord, here it is. I'm going to give you this debt. This is what they've done to me. I release it to You. I'm sowing it as seed faith in Your Kingdom, and I ask You to compensate me. I'm not going to get it from them, but I do ask You to compensate me."

I have every right to believe that, and I do! That way, I'm free from carrying around grudges, envy, jealousy, feelings of vengeance, and desire to get even. I don't want that cluttering my spirit. It's like garbage that you keep carrying around. Ultimately, it's going to affect your spirit.

Joseph was able to look back with hindsight

and see his life with all the devious roots that ultimately contributed to allowing him to be productive.

Joseph accomplished what God had raised him up to accomplish, to be the savior of the people of Egypt and of his own family.

The Apostle Paul wrote a letter to the Romans. In it he set forth truth in a most brilliant, concise, and wise way concerning our lives, God's will toward us, and the purpose of Jesus Christ in saving grace.

In the course of it he says, "Who shall deliver me from this body of death."[4]

Paul was referring to a custom in those days of dealing with premeditated murder and murderers. In their system of jurisprudence, when a man was found guilty and convicted of premeditated murder, they often gave him a very unique sentence.

When sentenced the murderer would be handcuffed with iron bands to the body of the person he murdered. Wherever the murderer went, he would then have to carry around the dead body of the person he killed.

Eventually by societal ostracism, family severance, and the weight of guilt in his own mind, the murderer would die by the burden he carried.

What the Apostle Paul referred to was the fact that we are burdened with the guilt of our sins. How will we ever find release from them?

Past sins were like an old dead body to be dragged around in life.

Then Paul makes the greatest of statements. "Thanks be unto Jesus Christ."[5]

When Jesus Christ forgives us of our sins, they are severed from us, never to be remembered against us again. God puts them away forever. Therefore, we are not to carry around the guilt of the past when it has been taken away by Jesus Christ.

Whatever the sins of the past may be, no matter how heinous or reprehensible, once they are forgiven and God has assured us in spirit and by His Word that they are all covered, we are never to be burdened with them again. That dead body of sin is gone.

Free.

Free from the past; free from guilt.

If God forgives us of our sins, and we do not forgive ourselves, then we make ourselves greater than God.

Not just *free from,* but *free to.*

Not just free from the guilt, but now free to love, free to work for the good of the one loved, free to serve and worship God, free to live the full life.

What glory there is in freedom.

We are called to obtain the glory of Jesus Christ.

Free in spirit.

Free in faith.

Free to believe God for all things.

That's the freedom Joseph enjoyed, and the freedom his brothers never knew.

There is joy in releasing our guilt through Jesus.

It's freedom.

Chapter 16

THE PRICE OF PEACE

To love someone is to work for their highest good.

Joseph loved his brothers. His love for them held the potential of their salvation. In the midst of famine, pestilence, and destitution, Joseph became the means of their salvation.

They accused him of not loving them when he reproved their sin. Not true. That was the very evidence of his love, but because of their perverted sense of right and wrong they failed to recognize it.

The command to repent may not seem loving to some, but it is the first word in a life of blessed unity with Jesus Christ and God our Father.

This book was not written simply to tell you that there are potential principles in life. Rather, I hope this book will stir you, move you, cause you to consider your ways, change where necessary, seek God if need be, and enable God to develop your life to the fullest.

People continually tell me, "Don't rock the boat," "Don't take risks," "Try to get along."

Personally, I'll leave that to the men who said it and let them wallow around in the morass of their own mediocrity.

One thing I have learned. Being nice is not always being loving.

I'm not talking about the nice that is courteous or gentlemanly. I mean that kind of nice that is bland, palliative, and so insipid that its sugar-coated sweetness seems artificial.

We're to be the salt of the earth, but if we have lost our savor, what good are we?

The kind of soft nice that I am talking about is best amplified by an encounter I had with a man who stopped me on my way to lunch and said he needed help. I had been busy all morning. I wanted to get a quick bite of food and get back to my office because I had a heavy afternoon schedule as well.

"This is important," he said. When I looked at him, I knew he meant it, and I passed up the lunch to be with him.

"I'm a mess," he stated. "I've attended a church for years, taught Sunday School, paid my tithes, done all the things I thought I was supposed to do.

"My wife and I had a good marriage, I thought. Not perfect you know, but good. Two years ago, she left me and got a divorce. She told me it was my fault because I had not been the kind

122

of husband I should have been. I tried to talk her out of it. I offered her anything and everything. I agreed to change my habits she did not like, but she refused and went ahead with the divorce.

"Since then I've really floundered. I've seen other women on two occasions, haven't gone to church, gone with some friends once to Las Vegas, and now I'm ready to go on vacation. I'm afraid of what will happen, what I'll do when I'm gone. When I heard you were here, Dr. Cole, I came looking for you because I need help. Now."

He meant it. I asked him about his wife.

"I really want her back. I'd do anything to get her back. It's been a long time, but it seems like yesterday."

"Where is she now?" I asked.

"She's remarried and has a child. After she left me, she went to work. Three weeks after the divorce, she was dating a man, became pregnant by him, then he divorced his wife, and they got married."

I looked at him in amazement.

"Was she going with that man when you were married," I had to know.

"Maybe she was. He was a good friend, and I thought he was counseling her. He did that sometimes for the pastor."

"Wait a minute," I said. "You mean your wife blamed you for the divorce, refused to be reconciled, committed adultery with her counselor, had his child, caused his divorce, and you still love her and want her back?"

"Well it was all my fault," he muttered.

"Your wife is a liar, an adulteress, a cheat, and a selfish person. Have you ever faced that fact?" I demanded.

"It's all my fault," he whispered again.

"Being nice to her by never facing her faults or sins has allowed her to make you the scapegoat and justify herself in her own eyes. Man, no wonder you're a mess. You're bearing her sins, his sins, their sins, your sins, and the guilt is killing you."

"What'll I do?" he asked earnestly.

"Face the issue. Reject her guilt. Admit her sin. Confess yours. Ask God for forgiveness. When God forgives you, forgive yourself. Renew your relationship with God through Christ. Get your life in line with the Word and get on with it. She emasculated your manhood, and you need to get it back."

We sat there for a while, then he asked me to pray with him. I did. I led him in a prayer while the Holy Spirit led him out of his quagmire of guilt and confusion.

The last I saw of him, he had a big smile, a big handkerchief wiping his eyes, and a big God who had just changed his life.

His being nice was not being loving. To her or to him.

Remorse and regret are not repentance.

In this day and time, we seem to be living in a worldwide happiness cult. Everybody has to be happy all the time, or they are not living a normal life. Churches in particular seem to be that way.

We segregate our sorrows. We put memorial services in funeral parlors, the sick in hospitals, and the infirm and mental patients in institutions.

Sorrow has the potential of being one of life's greatest teachers, producing some of life's greatest results.

Without sorrow for sin, there is no repentance. Without repentance there is no reconciliation, and without reconciliation there is no fellowship with God.

God chastens us because he loves us.[1]

Conviction of sin is not an evidence of God's displeasure but of His love. If He didn't make known to us what was wrong in our lives, we would never confess it out, and the sin left inside would prevent God's intimacy with us.

Recently a thief was shot in the foot by a car owner who saw the thief stealing from his car. A judge ruled that the owner of the car had to pay $40,000 to the thief for the injury sustained.

In Orange County, California, a man lost ninety days in jail for drunk driving while the parents of the child who was killed by him lost their child.

It's a perverted world.

A world where men who contend for righteousness and reprove unrighteousness are accused of being mean. Is it mean to wait until church is over to tell a man his house is on fire?

No wonder Peter preached to the multitude on the day of Pentecost and said, "Save yourself from this untoward generation."[2]

Or what about God's Word that says, "And have no fellowship with the unfruitful works of darkness, but rather reprove them."[3]

Why?

Peace and passivity are not synonymous.

God tells us to love our enemies, not to capitulate to them.

"Peace at any price" is devilish, not divine.

The truth when spoken must be spoken in love.

Joseph's love for his brothers was the potential for their ultimate good.

There is one supreme goal in every person's life. I don't care who it is, man, woman, boy, or girl. Each of us has a goal to have intimacy in a relationship. We can seek intimacy in our jobs, in our education, or with things.

But the ultimate goal of what you and I really seek after is some kind of intimacy that satisfies us personally. That means it has to be in a relationship.

God desires above all other things to have an intimate relationship with us.

Jesus Christ came to earth so that we could

be born into the Kingdom of God and have the Kingdom be born into us. He came so that we, through Him, might have a relationship with God that would stand the test of time and even eternity.

Intimacy is not developed by building barriers, constructing defenses, and closing our hearts, minds, and spirits.

In order to achieve intimacy, there needs to be an openness.

You can't have openness without vulnerability. Any time you close a door, you close yourself to vulnerability. But if you open the door, you become vulnerable.

Some people don't want to be vulnerable. If they have been hurt, they don't want to be hurt again. They can't stand the thought of being touched, being hurt. However, they want intimacy—but without openness or vulnerability. You can't get it that way.

You can't get intimacy through *religion*—only through a *relationship.*

Christianity is a loving relationship with a living God!

Intimacy then depends upon your dropping the defenses, dropping the barriers, and becoming more open and more vulnerable in order for that to happen.

It often means telling the truth in love and forgetting the saying of "peace at any price."

When Jesus met the woman at the well, she had her barriers up and her defenses up. She had her prejudices there. But the more Jesus talked to her, and the more she let down her guard, the more Jesus could reveal Himself to her. She went away from there rejoicing and telling everyone that she had found the Messiah.

Jesus said that if we lose our life for His sake, we'll find it.

If your principles for lifetime goals are not in line with God and His Word, it's time to rechart your direction.

PRINCIPLES FOR SUCCESS

Joseph was an overcomer.

He was an achiever in matters of the spirit.

He overcame prejudice, rejection, hostility, anxiety, despair, depression, and persecution. In the end, he triumphed over everything internally and externally. His enemies all lay at his feet, defeated.

It was Joseph's ability to submit, not his ability to resist, that enabled him to surmount it all. By submitting, he allowed God's transcendent glory to manifest itself in his life.

God's transcendent glory is revealed in His ability to take what was meant for evil, hurt, or harm, and turn it to our good when we commit it to Him.

Romans 8:28 tells us, "We know that all things work together for good to them that love God, to them who are the called according to his purpose."

If you are going through some of the things in your life that Joseph went through, then by submitting to God, you can have the same experiences that Joseph had.

If you are going through negative experiences, trials, and tribulations, remember that God never ends anything on a negative. He will always bring it around to the positive.

We are not to live a *crucified* life, but a *resurrected* life.

There is a colloquialism that says, "When the world gives you a lemon, make lemonade." Little does the world realize that this is based on a Kingdom principle. It is the *principle of transcendent glory*.

God has no plan for failure if your life is committed to Him.

Everything in life has potential, but it must be developed. It never develops itself. It's not how much you know, but how much you live up to what you know that determines success or failure in your life.

What you believe will determine how you relate to God and others. Each of us has weaknesses and strengths. Success comes by working through our strengths, not by dwelling on our weaknesses.

Words have creative power. We can create constructively or destructively. Balance is the key to life. You do not succeed in life by confessing things that are debilitating, degenerating, and depreciating. If God says you are a saint, then you need to confess that you are a saint. If God says you are a son of God, then you need to confess the fact that you are a son of God.

The purpose of Jesus Christ coming to earth was to become the image of God for the world to see. The image we have of God will either attract or repel us. If we have a poor image of ourselves, we cannot love ourselves or others as Scripture commands us to. *We need to create an image that will contribute to our own self-confidence.*

Everyone has a master passion. We either *master the passion or the passion masters us.* Satan has two weapons, temptation and accusation. If he can bring us under subjection to him by his accusations, he'll do it in order to keep us from the place of believing God and standing in righteousness before God. In righteousness, we have dominion over the devil and success in our life.

To Joseph, the honor of God was more important than his very own life. He suffered the loss of his reputation. He suffered the loss of his position. He suffered the loss of his possessions. He suffered the loss of everything he held dear, because to Joseph *some things in life were more important than life itself.*

True joy is born out of sorrow. If we will take our moment of crisis and commit it to God, He will turn it around and make it work for our good. That which is sorrowful to us now will ultimately end in joy. You can say to those who have offended or hurt you, after you have forgiven and released them, "God meant it to me for good."

Joseph was an overcomer. God wants us to be overcomers.

Lion's dens, fiery furnaces, and whale's bellies all have great potential because of God's ability to transcend every known circumstance into glory in your life.

May the life of Joseph be a testimony to you. May the teachings, the illustrations, the truths, the principles, and the patterns from his life all contribute to bringing potential success into your life.

It is my hope that you will apply these potential principles to all of your experiences where they are applicable.

Allow God, by His transcendent glory, to help you find or hold on to your dream.

In Joseph it is evident that God was always more concerned about his deliverance *to,* rather than his deliverance *from.* Same with Israel. God's purpose in taking Israel *out* was to bring them *into* Canaan. God's purpose in bringing Joseph *out* of his trials was to bring him *into* God's blessing.

God dealt with Joseph through every trial for thirteen years, but it equipped him to lead Egypt for eighty years.

Time is relative. You can live a lifetime in a few seconds or a few seconds can seem like a lifetime.

God's purpose in your life is to take everything in it and develop the potential of all of it by

His transcendent glory to bring ultimate glory to His name.

The fulfillment of your dream gives glory to God.

Your circumstances combined with God's power means *unlimited* potential success.

Trust Him.

It will be glory!

INDEX OF REFERENCES

Chapter 1
1. Hebrews 11:1
2. James 4:7
3. Proverbs 16:32
4. Titus 1:15
5. Acts 10:34

Chapter 2
1. Luke 2:52
2. Genesis 37:3
3. Psalm 1:1-3
4. Romans 1:17
5. Genesis 41:38
6. Proverbs 4:7

Chapter 3
1. John 6:9-11
2. Hebrews 11:3
3. Job 3:25

Chapter 5
1. *San Francisco Sunday Examiner and Chronicle,* May 22, 1983

Chapter 7
1. Mark 10:44
2. 1 Kings 3:25
3. James 5:7

Chapter 8
1. 1 John 1:9
2. Hebrews 1:3

Chapter 9
1. Judges 11:30-55
2. Matthew 14:6-9
3. Psalm 84:11

Chapter 10
1. James 1:14-15
2. Genesis 39:7
3. Genesis 39:14
4. Genesis 39:9
5. Matthew 9:4

Chapter 11
1. Matthew 11:6
2. Jonah 3:10; 4:1

Chapter 12
1. Genesis 50:20

Chapter 13
1. John 3:16
2. Genesis 25:29-33
3. 1 Samuel 2:22-25; 3:11-14
4. Mark 5:22-23

Chapter 14
1. Genesis 39:2
2. 1 Samuel 15:22
3. Luke 6:38
4. James 4:17

Chapter 15
1. Genesis 50:15
2. Genesis 50:17
3. Genesis 50:19
4. Romans 7:24
5. John 8:36

Chapter 16
1. Hebrews 12:6
2. Acts 2:40
3. Ephesians 5:11

ABOUT THE AUTHOR

Dr. Cole first ministered specifically to men during a men's retreat in 1980. At a conference in Pittsburgh later that same year, Dr. Cole spontaneously asked the congregation to pray that God would release him to a national ministry to men.

At another men's retreat, the Lord impressed Dr. Cole to "major in men," and people began to pray that God would bring 10,000 men to the rallies in 1981. That year, over 15,000 men attended the rallies, seminars, and meetings.

The substance of Dr. Cole's message became the backbone of his best-selling book, *Maximized Manhood*, which is in its fifth printing, with over 250,000 copies in print.

Over 300,000 men have been personally ministered to since that first men's retreat in Oregon, and thousands of lives have been changed.

Since February of 1984, the "Maximized Manhood" radio program has reached out to many men across the nation.